CHUZZLEWIT

Borgo Press Books by FRANK J. MORLOCK

Chuzzlewit: A Play in Two Acts
Falstaff: A Play in Four Acts (with William Shakespeare, John Dennis, and William Kendrick)
Outrageous Women: Lady Macbeth and Other French Plays (editor and translator)
The Stendhal Hamlet Scenarios and Other Shakespearean Shorts from the French (editor and translator)

CHUZZLEWIT
A PLAY IN TWO ACTS

FRANK J. MORLOCK

THE BORGO PRESS
MMXI

CHUZZLEWIT

Copyright © 2011 by Frank J. Morlock

FIRST EDITION

Published by Wildside Press LLC

www.wildsidebooks.com

DEDICATION

To the Memory of Fred Reinstein,

My friend and agent for many years,

Who really liked this play.

CONTENTS

CAST OF CHARACTERS	9
ACT I, Scene 1	11
ACT I, Scene 2	45
ACT II, Scene 3	69
ACT II, Scene 4	107
ACT II, Scene 5	123
ACT II, Scene 6	141
ABOUT THE AUTHOR	175

CAST OF CHARACTERS

Pecksniff, a Minister
Bailey, an Errand Boy
Jonas Chuzzlewit
Anthony C. (Chuzzlewit), Jonas's Father
Montague Tigg
Chevy Slyme
Mr. Spottletoe
A Cousin
Another Cousin
George Chuzzlewit
Cousin Two
Old Martin Chuzzlewit
Mr. Chuffy
Colonel Diver
Mr. Brick
Bellamy
Doctor Jobling
Charity, Pecksniff's Older Daughter
Mercy, Pecksniff's Younger Daughter
Maid at Todgers
Mrs. Spottletoe
A Young Lady
A Lady
Betsy Prig
Sarah Gamp
A Chamber Maid

ACT I
SCENE 1

Todgers.

A room in Mrs. Todgers' Rooming House. An improvised podium.

(Enter Maid, followed by Pecksniff.)

Pecksniff
Was everything prepared for the guests, young lady?

Maid (brightly)
Oh, yes, sir. I arranged everything special, sir. You see. (waves her hands about, indicating the chairs and speaker's podium.)

Pecksniff
Commendable! Very commendable, my dear girl. You are most deserving.

Maid (simpering)
I only do my best.

Pecksniff
You are a wonderful maid. A paragon of your profession. Your remarkable foresight, your address. Why, it's too much for

a poor man to express how marvelous you are. If I had a thousand tongues, and each one—

Maid
Oh, sir.

Pecksniff (sadly)
It saddens me that the rules of your estimable establishment forbid me to express my gratitude in a manner such as I might wish.

Maid
Begging your pardon, sir, I don't quite—

Pecksniff
You cannot accept—a gratuity, a token of my esteem, a munificence—in fine—a tip.

Maid
Oh, but—I mean, the rules aren't strictly—if no one is looking—

Pecksniff
No. (sadly) No, I cannot allow you to expose yourself to such a risk—for my sake. The very thought that you might be discharged.

Maid
Oh, dear.

Pecksniff
Released.

Maid
Oh.

Pecksniff
Turned out.

Maid
Oh.

Pecksniff
Because I—I had been so imprudent, so lacking in concern for the welfare of one who has placed me under infinite obligations—horrifies me to the extent that I—I—(struggling) I can't bring myself to do it. (wipes a tear from his eyes) Excuse me, excuse me. I must—(going)—when the guests come—call—call.

(Pecksniff exits. As he goes, Bailey enters, brushing by him.)

Pecksniff
Excuse me, my boy.

Bailey
Rather, so.

Maid
Bailey, excuse yourself to the gentleman.

Bailey
Shouldn't, his fault.

Maid
But he's a guest, Bailey.

Bailey
Can't see that makes any difference. What's he anyway?

Maid
Bailey, you grow more crude every day.

Bailey
Good wine ages, though. Don't it?

Maid (swings at him)
I'll age you.

Bailey (dodging deftly)
You'll age a good deal before you catch me.

Maid
Oh, behave. There are a lot of guests coming to see Mr. Pecksniff. Bailey, think how many nice tips you'll get.

Bailey
Doubtful, if they're at all like him.

Maid
What a thing to say. I've never seen a man more genteel.

Bailey
Oh, he tipped you, did he? Well, that's more than he did for me.

Maid
Not exactly. But, Bailey, he's so polite. So distinguished. And when you hear him talk. Why, he called me the—the "pentagon of my perfesshin"—now ain't that recumpinse, indeed?

Bailey
A six pence'd be better.

Maid
Get along with you.

Bailey
I ain't in no hurry.

Charity (outside)
Oh, maid. Where are you? (enters) Oh, here you are. Will you favor me by taking this box to my father?

Maid
Why, certainly, ma'am.

Charity
How can I thank you?

Bailey (to Maid, low)
I kin tell how she ain't.

Charity
I wonder how my father can stand all these low people. They know nothing. And, what's worse they have nothing—and they're never where you want them, when you want them. Ah, it's very vexing for a girl of my temperament, by nature easy, carefree—and never angry when things are the way I expect them.

Mercy (enters)
Oh, Charity, is it you?

Charity
Do I look like someone else? Don't be stupid.

Mercy
Oh, are you off again? Well, all I want to know is, what can we do while father presides over this conclave of the Chuzzlewit clan?

Charity
Do? We must help him.

Mercy
Help him—like hell! When I'm in London, I intend to do something.

Charity
Don't you think I feel the same? But, we've got to help. You know he can be a Tartar at times.

Mercy
Don't I ever. But, what's the sense in this meeting? Is it a family reunion or what?

Charity
Oh, Mercy, don't you know? With your faculty for eavesdropping?

Mercy
My faculty for—of all the—

Charity
Sister, sister, don't offend these pristine walls with the reverberations of irreverent blasphemous sounds.

Mercy
You. (Oh, never mind.) Why are we here? You mean our American uncle?

Charity
Just the one.

Mercy
Is he going to be here?

Charity
No.

Mercy
Oh! I heard he was rich. I thought, perhaps, he might like to have a young niece to look after him, help him—

Charity
Spend his money.

Mercy
Exactly.

Charity
It would be nice.

Mercy
Well, if he isn't coming, what's everybody here for?

Charity
Martin Chuzzlewit is dying.

Mercy
What a shame.

Charity
And, supposedly, he intends to leave his money to charity.

Mercy
To you!?

Charity
No, stupid. To some institution to clothe Indian orphans.

Mercy
And disinherit his own relatives? That dirty—

Charity
And Daddy proposed this meeting of all his next-of-kin to

suggest that somebody be sent to Uncle Martin to bring him to his senses.

Mercy
But, do you think—after all, America's a long way away.

Charity
But his disease is a lingering one.

Mercy
And we'll send—

Mercy and Charity
Daddy.

Bailey
I heard you're leaving? Worse luck.

Mercy
But, who told you?

Bailey
A little bird.

Mercy
Cherry, darling, I think you have a secret admirer in Bailey here.

Charity
Bailey, you mustn't eavesdrop.

Bailey
Oh, no, ma'am, not at all. You ain't going to leave the young men there a lock of your hair, are you? It's real, ain't it?

Charity
You go too far—

Mercy
Of course, *mine* is real—

Bailey
Oh, it is "of course" though? (in a whisper) Hers, ain't. I seen it hanging on the nail by the winder. Besides, I pulled it once. She never knowed!

Mercy
You must leave my sister alone.

Bailey
I'm a-going to leave, anyway. I ain't a-going to stand being called names by Mrs. Todgers no longer.

Mercy
But, what will you do?

Bailey
There's soldiers in the Tower. I'm acquainted with 'em. Don't their country set a value on 'em, mind you? Not at all!

Charity
You might be shot. (brightly) But I'm not trying to discourage you. It simply occurred to me. Do join.

Bailey
Well, wot if I am shot? I'd sooner be shot than hit by a rolling pin. Wot, wot, if the gentlemen do consume the pervershins? It ain't my fault if their appetizers is good, is it?

Mercy
No one says so.

Bailey
Don't they, though! No! One mayn't say so, but some one knows so. I ain't a-giving to have every rise in prices visited upon me. I ain't a- going to be killed because of a rise in the economic cycle. So you'd better give me whatever you mean to give me, becos if you ever come back, I shan't be here. As to the other boy, he won't deserve any, nothing.

Charity
Why, then, from all of us—

Bailey
The story always works. Like a charm.

Charity
I feel honored to present you with this.

Bailey (stares stupidly at the gift)
I ain't sure I can pay you back for this.

Charity
Don't think of repayment, Bailey.

Bailey
But, I am going to think of it. I ain't going to forget it. I'll pay you back in coin.

(Bailey exits.)

Mercy
Really, he is a good boy.

Charity
Perhaps, I might have given him sixpence. Would that have been too extravagant?

Mercy
What did you think?

Charity
I fear it was.

(Reenter Bailey.)

Bailey
A gintleman to see Miss Charity!

(Charity looks to Mercy. Bailey makes a terrible face and shakes his fist in token of revenge to come.)

Charity
For me? My gracious.

Bailey
Ah, it is my gracious, ain't it? Wouldn't I be gracious neither if I was him!

Charity
But, I don't know any gentlemen. He must be mistaken. Who can it be?

Mercy
A very ridiculous person, I'm sure.

Charity
I don't see he's so ridiculous.

Mercy
I've very much at ease on that score.

Charity
Jealousy in a sister. Your head is turned.

Mercy

Yes. Men keep me spinning so much. I'm in a whirl. It's much nicer to be like you, Charity. So free from the odious creatures. How do you do it?

Charity (savagely whispering)

I'll settle you later.

(Mercy smiles with perfect tranquility and exits. Enter Jonas.)

Jonas

Here I am, you see, cousin. How are you?

Charity

Why, just fine, cousin Jonas. How did you know we were in London?

Jonas

Why, some one told me so, naturally. How's the other one?

Charity

Mercy? Why don't you ask her about it?

Jonas

No hurry. There's no occasion for that, you know. What a cruel girl you are.

Charity

Me? How did I ever give you cause to think that?

Jonas

You ain't even asked where I've been. I say—did you think I was lost?

Charity

I never considered the possibility.

Jonas
Didn't you, though? How about the other one? Did the other one?

Charity
Never to me.

Jonas
Didn't she even laugh about it?

Charity
No!

Jonas
She's a terrible one to laugh, ain't she?

Charity
Very lively, my sister.

Jonas
Liveliness is a pleasant thing, when it don't lead to spending money. Ain't it?

Charity
Ever so pleasant.

Jonas
Such as yours, I mean, you know. By the way, how's the old hypocrite?

Charity (wounded)
He's my father.

Jonas
Egad, but, you may say what you like about my father. I give you leave. I think liquid aggravation circulates through his

veins, not regular blood. How old should you think he is?

Charity
Nice and old.

Jonas
My foot. It's time he was *drawn* out a little nicer. He's over eighty, you know.

Charity
Who would ever think so? You're so lucky.

Jonas
Lucky! Egad, I don't see much hope of his dying before he's a hundred. If he had any feeling for me, he'd of died long ago. He should be ashamed of himself, disappointing his only son like this. What's his religion I should like to know, when he goes flying in the face of the Bible like that! But, I came to invite you for a walk and to stop at the house. I say, you'll bring the other one, you know—

(Enter Mercy.)

Jonas
Ah, there you are, are you?

Mercy
Yes, fright—but I could much rather be anywhere else, I assure you.

Jonas
You don't mean that. You can't, you know. It isn't possible.

Mercy
You can have your opinion, fright, I have mine. And I am contented with it. In my opinion, fright, you are a very

unpleasant, odious, nasty person. (laughs)

Jonas
Oh, you're a sharp gal! She's a regular teaser, ain't she, cousin?

Charity
I am sure I don't know what a teaser is. It wouldn't be ladylike to have one for a sister. Nor admit it, whatever her real nature may be!

(Enter Pecksniff.)

Pecksniff
If it was possible to find any source for this merriment, I should reprove you, but—

Jonas
I don't care for that; I don't care that (snaps his fingers) for you, old hypocrite. Don't suppose I do.

Pecksniff
Why, cousin Jonas. This explains the merriment.

Jonas (to Charity)
I should think no more of admitting daylight into this fellow than if he was a bellboy. You don't have a mind to be an heiress, do you, cousin? If so—

Pecksniff
Bless you, my child, bless you. We rarely receive family calls. And, how is your respected father, my dear cousin Anthony?

Jonas (with complete disgust)
Healthy. In fact, living with no reasonable prospect of ending my sufferings.

Pecksniff
How wonderful for you.

Jonas
Are you being funny? (to Charity) Let him beware!

Pecksniff (rather put off by the rudeness)
Well, business is good, I trust?

Jonas
I don't think I care to commit myself on that.

Charity
Papa, Jonas came to visit me.

Pecksniff
My little Charity has an admirer? (beams)

Mercy
It is unexpected, isn't it, pa? But then, what can you expect of a fright like this?

Pecksniff
Mercy your manners. Jonas I want you to feel welcome, very welcome.

Mercy
Yes, Papa has waited a long time—

Jonas
Enough's enough. I refuse to stand here and be insulted by him! Cousin, and the other one, goodbye. I shall come again when the old hypocrite ain't in.

Mercy
Exit a monster.

(Jonas smiles at her.)

Jonas
Not by him!

Pecksniff
What a very rude young man. Well he need never fear good manners will be his undoing. Why, Cherry, my dear.

Charity (crying)
He came to see me. Did you have to offend him?

Pecksniff
But I tried to avoid it.

Charity
My first gentleman caller.

Pecksniff
But, what could I do?

Charity
Oh Papa, don't be such a hypocrite.

Pecksniff
But Cherry—

Charity
Hoo, waah, hoo, hooh, hoo—!

(Pecksniff goes to the door and opens door out and knocks over Montague Tigg.)

Pecksniff
My good man, what are you doing with your eye so close to the keyhole. Let it be a lesson to you sir, a moral lesson.

Montague Tigg
Stay! Wait a bit. What then?

Pecksniff
Vagabond. Do you know this is a private establishment? Where there are LADIES present. What then indeed, sir?

Montague
Wait a bit. You are—you are Reverend Seth Pecksniff, D.D.

Pecksniff
I am. Minister of the Gospel

Montague (pulling his shirt collar to visibility)
You behold sir one who has an interest in these affairs.

(Montague pulls documents from his dirty hatband.)

Montague
Peruse. You know Chevy Slyme, I believe?

Pecksniff
I have heard of the miserable sinner.

Montague
That, sir, is my reason and interest here.

Pecksniff
It distresses me to be compelled to call you a liar; you are not he. No, I don't excuse you—

Montague
Stop. Wait a bit. I understand your mistake. I am not offended. Why? Because it's complimentary. You suppose I set myself up for Chevy Slyme? Sir, if there is a man on earth whom a gentleman would feel proud and honored to be mistaken for,

that man is Chevy Slyme.

Pecksniff
Sir!

Montague (paying no attention)
For he is, without an exception, the highest minded, the most independent spirited, the most original, spiritual, classical, talented, the most thoroughly Shakespearean, if not Miltonic, and at the same time, the most disgustingly unappreciated dog I know! But, sir, I have not the vanity to attempt to pass for Slyme. Any other man in the wide world, I am equal to; but Slyme is, I frankly confess, a great many cuts above me. (sententiously) Therefore, you are wrong.

Pecksniff
How could I make such a mistake?

Montague
The whole thing resolves itself into an instance of the peculiarities of genius.

Pecksniff
Indeed.

Montague
Yes, every man of genius has peculiarities and the peculiarity of my friend Slyme is that he is always waiting around the corner.

Pecksniff
You say so!

Montague
It is a remarkable and curiously interesting trait in Slyme's character; whenever Slyme's life comes to be written, that trait

must be thoroughly worked out or society will not be satisfied. Observe me, sir, society will not be satisfied.

Pecksniff
I do, indeed, with marvel.

Montague
Slyme's biographer, whoever he may be, must apply to me; or, if I am gone, to that what's-his-name from which nothing remarkable returns. He must search my notes, notes I have recorded of that great man's proceedings, my adopted brother, sir—which would amaze you.

Pecksniff
More and more.

Montague
He made use of an expression, an expression, sir, observe me, only the 15th of last month, when he couldn't meet a little bill—which would have done honor to Napoleon Bonaparte addressing his army.

Pecksniff
Sir, sweet sir. I beg your pardon, but what the hell do you want?

Montague
Sir, my name, allow me to introduce myself, is Tigg. Montague Tigg. The name is familiar? No? It was my father's name. Distinguished in the peninsula wherefore I am proud, yes, I am proud. Proud as Lucifer.

Pecksniff
The point!

Montague
Slyme.

(Enter Slyme furtively.)

Montague
Now, sir. You are related. Relations never agree. A wise dispensation, or there would be none but family parties. If you were on good terms, I should consider you a most confoundedly unnatural pair; but, as I look upon you as a couple of devilishly deep-thoughted fellows who may be reasoned with to any extent—

(Slyme doesn't say a word, but nudges Tigg.)

Montague
Chiv, I shall come to that presently. I act upon my own responsibility or not at all. To the extent of a loan of a crown piece to a man of your talents. I look upon Mr. Pecksniff as certain. You see, Mr. Pecksniff, it is one of the peculiarities of genius to always be in want. Oh, Chiv. You are, upon my life, a strange instance of little frailties that beset a mighty mind. If there had never been a telescope in the world, I should have been quite certain from my observation of you that there were spots on the Sun.

Pecksniff
You have a remarkable talent of observation. Remarkable.

Montague
As Hamlet says, Hercules—ah, what was it Hamlet says? Pity, I've lost my train. Ah. Life's a riddle. But, there's no use in talking about it. Ha. Ha.

Pecksniff
None, I see.

Montague
But, there's consolation. Yes, consolation. We can do good to

each other. Now I'm a most confoundedly soft-hearted fellow, and I can't stand by and see you two blades cutting each others' throats when there's nothing to be got by it. You're a cousin. We are cousins, but you can't get at him, neither can we. No, suppose, sir, you buy Chiv out.

Pecksniff
I may feel my cousin does not regard me with exactly that amount of Christian love which should subsist between us. But he may regulate his affairs, but consider as he chooses. Sir, what is there to buy out?

Montague
Why, as to that, it is a difficult question.

Pecksniff
One I don't feel I have a right to discuss.

Montague
Did you know the Spottletoes are here?

Pecksniff
What's that you say!

Slyme (sulkily)
The one that married my father's brother's child. She was a favorite once.

Pecksniff
Dreadful. She was a rapacious woman.

Slyme
Anthony Chuzzlewit has got wind of it, too. Your scheme of getting all the relatives that can be trusted together to sell out or send you to represent them in America is very clever, but it won't work. Buy us, or we go to them.

Pecksniff
Oh.

Montague
This is the point I was gradually arriving at when my friend Slyme here, with his typical genius, cut the Gordian Knot.

(Slyme retreats.)

Montague
We must not be too hard on the eccentricities of our friend Slyme. Five Shillings? Very moderate. Extraordinarily generous of him, and I never knew that man to fail to redeem a promise. You're not in want of change are you? I could run and get—

Pecksniff
No.

Montague
Perhaps you'd rather not lend Slyme five shillings. Would you entertain the same objection to lending me five shillings?

Pecksniff
No. Other objections.

Montague
Why then, we come to the ridiculously small sum of eight pence.

Pecksniff
And that is equally objectionable.

Montague
Sir, you are one of the most consistent and remarkable men I have ever met. Allow me. (shakes his hand) There are, you see, eccentricities about Slyme I can never quite approve,

for all his genius. But, I can forgive him these for having brought me into the presence of you. It is one of the most delightful experiences I have ever had. I must run. You will excuse me. Ladies. Mr. Pecksniff. (exits)

Pecksniff and His Daughters
Ha, ha, ha.

Mercy
What a way of talking.

(Enter the Spottletoes, Anthony C. and Jonas, and others, and reenter Slyme.)

Mrs. Spottletoe (a queer little woman, very frail)
Ah, there you are, Pecksniff. Now, what's all this nonsense? You expect me to drag myself all the way to London, just to—? Me, with my political constitution?

Pecksniff
Lovely, Martha. You are well? And here comes Anthony Chuzzlewit and little Jonas. Why, how big you've grown, Jonas.

Jonas
Yeah. (Jonas is around forty) Save your gushing for someone who is deceived by it.

Anthony
That's my boy. Tell him, Jonas.

Jonas
Old hypocrite.

Pecksniff
I'll pray for you, Jonas.

(Several other people enter, about a half dozen in all. Slyme returns with Montague.)

Pecksniff
Well, and are we all here and comfortable? How very nice. How wonderful it is to see the family reunited. It does me good to see it. It does my daughters good. We thank you. Gratitude fills our hearts for this blessing you have conferred upon us. We shall not easily forget.

Spottletoe
Sorry to interrupt, Pecksniff, but what makes you think we are here to confer an honor upon you?

Everyone
Hurray!

Spottletoe
I am no stranger to your desire to be regarded as the head of the family, but I can tell you, sir—

Pecksniff
Apparently you have your own aspirations.

(Spottletoe is hissed down.)

Pecksniff
I am not sorry for this incident. No. It is meet that we speak frankly, if not courteously.

A Young Lady
It would be nice if some were frank. If only for the novelty, and, as for the insinuation that my hair is not my own, I scorn it. It certainly belongs more to me than honesty does to some that I could name. Or their hair, for that matter.

Charity
Was that low observation meant for me, *miss*?

A Young Lady
If it wasn't, it shouldn't bother you.

Charity
You are making yourself very ridiculous.

A Cousin
Now, really, Miss. Ladies.

Another Cousin
Don't you call my daughter a lady. I'll kick you to pieces for a halfpenny.

Pecksniff
Please, everyone, please. It's to be lamented that this has occurred. But, the Lord will give us the—

Anthony
Pecksniff, don't.

Pecksniff
Don't...?

Anthony
Don't be such a hypocrite.

Pecksniff
Charity, remind me to pray more particularly for Chuzzlewit's soul tonight. He has done me an injustice. (beginning again) All our thoughts centering on our dearly beloved relative that circumstances have placed beyond our reach—we are met to see, if by any justifiable means—

Lady
In such a case as this, necessity knows no law.

Pecksniff
By <u>any</u> means to open the eyes of our relative from his present infatuation. Whether it is possible to reveal the true character of the young woman who has cast a shadow of disgrace over this family. She has persuaded him to leave his property to charity. What else might she persuade him to do? This is the first step in a concerted effort to deprive us, his next-of-kin, of our fair share of eighteen million pounds.

Lady
Poison her.

Mrs. Spottletoe
Scalp her. Give her to the Redskins.

Mercy
Bridewell.

Charity
Flogging.

Montague
This is no way to treat a lady. (offends the misses Pecksniff) You are positively too harsh, my girls, upon my soul. And you are too hard on me. (sighs)

Pecksniff
I won't say she deserves these punishments, but God save me, I can't say she doesn't. Something must be done to stop her.

Charity
Go on, Pa.

Pecksniff
We must stop this godless, alluring, pagan, sir—sir—

Cousin
Swain!

Cousin Two
Oyster.

Pecksniff
No. A Siren. We must prevent her.

Lady
If Mr. George Chuzzlewit has anything to say to me, I beg him to speak out like a man and not look at me as if he could eat me.

George
A cat can look at a king. And, I hope I, as a member of the family, can look at one who has only come into it by marriage. As to eating, I am not a cannibal, and besides, I have very sensitive digestion.

Lady
I don't know about that.

George
For, if I was a cannibal, I should think a lady who has outlived three husbands must be uncommonly tough.

Lady
You bastard!

George
And, I will further add, I think it much more becoming if those who intruded themselves into this family by getting on

the blind side of some of its members before marriage and manslaughtering them afterwards would refrain from acting like vultures to those members of the family now living.

Lady
I was prepared for this from the first.

George
And I will further add, it would be more seemly if those individuals would stay home and be content with their spoils, rather than hovering about thrusting their fingers into the family pie which they flavor enough from fifty miles off, I can tell them.

Lady
What else could I expect from a herd of vixens like this?

Charity
Don't direct your halfpenny officer's look at me.

Lady
I passed from the memory of a noble family when I married into this one. I lost my claim upon the United Kingdom and Ireland, I so degraded myself. Now, my dears, having improved yourself by the example of these genteel young ladies, we'll go.

Montague (miffed)
Oh, please don't.

Lady
Mr. Pecksniff, we came to be entertained. You have outdone our justified expectation. Thank you.

(They sweep out. Reenter Spottletoe.)

Spottletoe
Now, Pecksniff, what's the meaning of this? Read this letter. Friends, it appears our dear relative is very ill. He asks those of us who can to come to America. He hasn't made his will yet. He says he wants to see us all. Deny, Pecksniff, that you didn't bring us here to hide it from us. To cheat us. Deny it, deny it. To cheat us. Deny it, deny it.

Pecksniff
But, this is quite news to me.

Montague
But, the duplicity of this is marvelous. Remarkable. Pecksniff, I congratulate you. You are one of the most remarkable and consistent men I have ever met. Can't be bought this time, Pecksniff. We're going to America.

Anthony
And so are we.

Jonas
Outsmarted yourself, old hypocrite.

Pecksniff
It is not my desire to wound the feelings of any person with whom I am connected in family bonds. I may be a hypocrite, but I am not a brute.

Anthony
Pooh, pooh! What signifies that word, Pecksniff? Hypocrite? Why, we are all hypocrites. I am sure I feel that to be agreed among us or I shouldn't have come. Not one of us would be here if we were not hypocrites.

Jonas
You see, Pecksniff.

Anthony
But, the annoying thing about you is that you would deceive everybody, just as if you really believed yourself.

Pecksniff
How honesty is maligned.

Jonas
I'd lay a handsome wager now, if I ever laid a wager, which I don't, and never will, that you keep up appearances before your own daughters, here.

Anthony
You're not offended.

Pecksniff (beaming)
It's hard to offend me.

Jonas
Can't you see it flatters the old hypocrite?

Anthony (buttonholing Pecksniff)
Where's the use of division between you and me? We are two halves of a pair of scissors, but together we are something. Eh?

Pecksniff
Unanimity is always delightful.

Anthony
Can't say that. There are some people I would rather differ than agree with. You know my opinion of you.

Pecksniff (agonized)
Hypocrite.

Anthony
Complimentary, complimentary, upon my word. It was an involuntary tribute to your abilities.

Pecksniff
I am cruelly misunderstood, but I shall not complain.

Anthony
Jonas is a shrewd lad.

Pecksniff
He would seem so.

Anthony
And careful.

Pecksniff
And careful, I have no doubt.

Anthony
Look ye. I think he is sweet upon your daughter.

Pecksniff
Young people.

Anthony
Jonas ain't young.

Pecksniff
But cousins generally fall in love.

Anthony
We never did. But, supposing they are in love. *We* have interest to protect. Stop. I know what you would say. Unnecessary. You haven't thought of this. Your dear child's happiness. Your paternal responsibilities. You don't care to commit

yourself. Yes, quite right. And like you! But we can't ignore this. One of us might be placed at a disadvantage. I shall not occupy that position. Now that we both know it and see it, we shall both pretend not to know it or see it, which is agreeable to us both, I am sure.

BLACKOUT/CURTAIN

ACT I
SCENE 2

Jonas at home.

Jonas
Well, ghost. Is dinner nearly ready?

Anthony
I should think it was.

Jonas
What's the good of that? I should think it was. I want to know.

Anthony
Ah. I don't know for certain.

Jonas
You don't know for certain? No, you don't know for certain, you don't. Give me the candle there. I want it for the gals. Bachelor's hall, you know, cousins. I say—the other one will be having a laugh at this when she gets home, hey, won't she. Here you sit on the right side of me and I'll have her on my left. Other one, will you come here?

Mercy
You're such a fright, you'll take my appetite. But I suppose I must.

Jonas
Ain't she lively.

(Jonas digs Charity in the ribs.)

Charity
Oh, I don't know!

Jonas
What's that precious old father of mine doing now? What are you looking for?

Anthony
I've lost my glasses, Jonas.

Jonas
Sit down without your glasses, can't you? You don't eat or drink out of 'em, I think. Where's the sleepy-headed Chuffy got to? Now, stupid. Oh, you know your name, do you? Our clerk, Old Chuffy.

Mercy
Is he deaf?

Jonas
No, I don't know that he is. He ain't deaf, is he, father?

Anthony
I never heard him say that he was.

Mercy
Blind?

Jonas
N-no. I never understood that he was at all blind. You don't consider him so, do you, father?

Anthony
Certainly, not.

Charity
What is he, then?

Jonas
Why, I'll tell you what he is. He's precious old for one thing, and I ain't best pleased with him for that, for I think my father must have caught it of him. He's a strange old chap for another—and don't understand anyone hardly, but him. (pointing to his father with a fork)

Mercy
Strange.

Jonas
A long while ago. We don't do much business now, and he ain't a bad clerk. A very good one. Well! He ain't a dear one, at all events. He hardly understands anyone except my father. He always understands him though, and wakes up quite wonderful.

Mercy
He doesn't seem to like his food.

Jonas
Oh, yes, he eats when he's helped. And he don't care whether he waits a minute or an hour, so long as father's here. No, Chuffy Stupid, are you ready?

(Chuffy remains immovable.)

Jonas
Always a perverse old file.

Anthony
Are you ready for your dinner?

Chuffy
Yes, yes. Yes, yes. Quite ready, Mr. Chuzzlewit, quite ready, sir. All ready, all ready.

Jonas
He'll be very disagreeable, mind. He always chokes himself when it ain't broth. Look at him now! Did you ever see a horse with such a wall-eyed expression as he's got. If it hadn't been for the joke of it, I wouldn't have let him come in today, but I thought he'd amuse you.

Mercy
You have a wonderful sense of humor.

Jonas
Other one, glad you like it.

Mercy
I expected it of you.

Jonas
Better peck away at your bread, Chuffy.

Chuffy
Aye, aye, quite right, quite right. He's your own son, Mr. Chuzzlewit; bless him for a sharp lad. Bless him. Bless him.

Jonas
One of these days Chuffy will be the death of me. (pours for the ladies) Don't spare it. Plenty more where it came from—err, don't take that too seriously, I'm just joking.

Anthony

I shall drink to Pecksniff. Your father, my dears. A clever man Pecksniff. A wary man! A hypocrite though, eh? A hypocrite, girls, eh? Ha, ha, ha. Well, so he is. Now, among friends, he is. I don't think the worse of him for that unless it is that he overdoes it. You may overdo anything, my darlings. You may overdo even hypocrisy. Ask Jonas.

Jonas

You can't overdo taking care of yourself. (pointedly, but with his mouth full)

Anthony

Wisdom, my dears. I taught him. I trained him. Jonas is the heir of my upbringing. I worked for this. I hoped for this. It has been the great end of my life.

Jonas (whispers to Chuffy)

Except, except when one lives too long. Ha, ha. Tell the other one that.

Chuffy

Your own son, Mr. Chuzzlewit.

Charity

Tell her yourself, can't you?

Jonas

She seems to make such a game of one.

Charity

Well, then, don't bother with her. She doesn't bother herself about you, I'm sure.

Jonas

Don't she, though! That don't break my heart. Come a little

closer.

Charity
Shh.

Jonas
Don't mind crowding me. I like to be crowded by gals. Come a little closer, cousin.

(Charity, with the most fantastic series of darting looks at the others at the table, slowly but surely manages to get quite close to Jonas.)

Anthony
What a cold spring it is.

Jonas
You don't have to go scorching your clothes into holes, whether it is or not. Broadcloth stopped ain't so cheap as that comes to.

Anthony
A good lad! A prudent lad. He never delivered himself up to vanities of dress. No, no.

Jonas
I don't know, but I would, though mind you, if I could do it for nothing. Don't go poking at the fire. Do you mean to come to want in your old age?

Anthony
No time for that. I wish there was.

Jonas
You always were as selfish an old blade as need be. You act up to your character. You wouldn't mind coming to want,

wouldn't you? I dare say you wouldn't. And your own flesh and blood might come to want, too, might they for anything you cared? Oh, you precious old flint. There isn't time. No, I should hope not, but you'd live to be a couple of hundred, if you could. And after all be discontented. I know you.

Anthony
Going to die, Jonas.

Jonas (shaking his spoon at him and surreptitiously nudging Charity)
If you're in such a state of mind as that, why don't you make over your property. Buy an annuity cheap. And make your life interesting to yourself and everybody else that watches the speculation. But that couldn't suit you. That would be natural conduct to your own son and you like to be unnatural and to keep him out of his rights. Why, I should be ashamed of myself if I was you and glad to hide my head in the what-you-may-call-it.

Chuffy
He's your own son, Mr. Chuzzlewit. Your own son, sir.

Anthony
A chip off the old block, Chuffy.

Jonas
Precious old.

Chuffy
No, no, no. Not old at all, sir.

Jonas
He's worse than ever you know. He's getting too bad. Hold your tongue, will you?

Anthony
He says you're wrong. (to Chuffy)

Chuffy
Tut, tut. I know better. I say he's wrong. I say he's wrong. He's a boy. So are you, Mr. Chuzzlewit. Don't mind him.

Anthony
I grow deaf.

Chuffy
But, what if you do? I've been deaf this twenty years.

Anthony
I grow blinder, too.

Chuffy
That's a good sign. Ha, ha, the best sign in the world. You saw too well before.

Jonas (to Charity)
They've been carrying on this game for the last two or three weeks. I never saw my father take so much notice of him before. What! You're legacy hunting are you, Mr. Chuffy? Eh? (waves his fist near his face)

Charity
I think your father is asleep.

Jonas
Why, so he is. It would be nice if I could store that peripatetic fortune my father represents in a strong box—vulgarly called a coffin. What are parents good for?

Charity
Oh, but I love my father. I always feed him well.

Jonas
Do you? Is that economical?

Charity
But, fat people go quickly.

Jonas
God, I never thought of that. (Anthony groans) He has the nightmare. Do you have the nightmare, cousin?

Charity
Oh, never.

Jonas
Does the other one? Does she ever have the nightmare?

Charity (moves away)
Ask her yourself.

Mercy
Only when I look at you, cousin.

Jonas
She laughs so there is no talking to her. She's wild. I saw the wilderness in her t'other day. But you're the one to sit prim, cousin.

Charity (simpering and rubbing against him like a cat)
Am I?

(A knock at the door.)

Jonas
Who can that be? Ah, it's your father.

(Charity sits prim and quite far away. Jonas goes out and returns with Pecksniff.)

Jonas
What are you prying and peering about here for? It's precious odd.

Pecksniff
I have business with your father. Ah, Mercy and Charity. Why, you wag, Jonas.

Jonas
I suppose then can come and go as they please.

Pecksniff
Why, of course. I am delighted they came. But, my dears, you must go to Todgers now. I have to talk business.

Mercy
We won't mind.

Charity
You couldn't have come more opportunely, father. (frigidly)

(They go out after appropriate bows. Mercy makes a face at Jonas. He scowls. Charity simpers.)

Jonas
Hallo, father, here's Pecksniff! He gets more addlepated every day. (shaking him) Don't I tell you Pecksniff's here, stupid head?

Anthony
Hi, hi. Oh, Pecksniff's here.

Pecksniff
And, would you be so kind as to see my girls home, Mr. Jonas.

Jonas
I'm on to you, Pecksniff. I—

Pecksniff
Don't you want to see them home?

Jonas
I did. But now, I don't.

Pecksniff
Pish. It's a sly man will outwit you, Jonas, but really, I must insist.

Jonas
Oh, very well, Pecksniff. But, remember, I'll send for the carriage.

(Jonas goes.)

Pecksniff
Now we are alone. I indulge in that presumption because our dear friend Mr. Chuffy is what is called—metaphysically speaking—a dummy.

Anthony
He neither hears us nor sees us.

Pecksniff
When I received your letter—I was astonished, gratified. The confidence you propose to include me in—moves me, overcomes me.

Anthony
No doubt you were gratified.

Pecksniff
That one you did a verbal injury should.

Anthony
Will you hold your tongue, sir, and let me speak? Jonas is sweet upon your daughter.

Pecksniff
A father's pride.

Anthony
You know better. You lie! What, you will be a hypocrite, will you? If your daughter was what you would have me think, she would never do for Jonas. Never. I wouldn't consider her. But she is a mean, stingy bitch. Exactly the woman for Jonas. She will not run riot. She is too ugly to be unfaithful. No. She is ideal.

Pecksniff
My dear Anthony.

Anthony
Pecksniff—be quiet for once. I am worth a few million, Pecksniff. You are, too. So is our American relative, Old Martin. We live like pigs. Why? Because we had to live like pigs to get this money. We will never let it go. The fever of acquisition has consumed us. Well I take that fever with me to the grave. I can't bear the thought all I made will be wasted. So, therefore, Pecksniff, a mean stingy bitch for Jonas. It's my only consolation.

Pecksniff
You speak only—

Anthony
Come here! Jonas will be my heir; Jonas will be rich, and a

great catch for you. Your daughter comes of a good hard-grasping stock.

Pecksniff
Is there any more you want to say?

Jonas (enters)
Sorry, Pecksniff, long enough. Can't have you getting yourself a legacy. (He goes to the cabinet with the will.) See there I am. Still there, Pecksniff. I say, Pecksniff—now that your here there's something I want to talk to you about.

Pecksniff
Is there? Feel free, my boy.

Jonas
How much of a portion do you intend to give your daughters?

Pecksniff
That's a very singular inquiry.

Jonas
Now don't you mind whether it's singular or plural but answer it or let it alone. One or the other.

Pecksniff
What would I give them, eh?

Jonas
What would you give them?

Pecksniff
That depends upon the husbands? My standards in sons-in-law is high. *You* have spoilt me and made it a fanciful one, an imaginative one—a tinged one, a sterling one.

Jonas
Is it? I should hope it was sterling. Lots.

Pecksniff
Supposing I were to get such a son-in-law as you.

Jonas
Supposing you were to get such a son-in-law as me. What then?

Pecksniff
I should go to the very limit of my means. And well I know whose husband you would be.

Jonas
Whose? (dry)

Pecksniff
Charity, my eldest. I must one day part with her. I am prepared for it.

Jonas
Ecod, you've been prepared for that for a pretty long time I should think.

Pecksniff
Yes, she has not been as cherry of late perhaps.

Jonas
I suppose you'll have to part with the other one—one of these days.

Pecksniff
In time she'll tame down. But Cherry, Mr. Jonas, Cherry—

Jonas
Oh, age has made her all right enough. But you haven't answered

what I asked you. Of course you're not obliged to do it you know if you don't like.

Pecksniff
It would pinch and cramp me but I—I would bestow on either girl. For such a son-in-law as you.

Jonas
Done, Father. What? My father asleep again. Ah, and snoring. Only hear!

Pecksniff
He snores very deep. Do you know, Jonas, I think your father is—breaking.

Jonas
Oh, is he though? Ecod, you don't know how tough he is. He ain't upon the move yet. Oh, the other one, are you back?

Charity
The carriage hasn't come.

Mercy
My goodness, you here, fright. Well I'm very thankful you won't trouble me much.

Jonas
What. You're as lively as ever are you. Oh, you're a wicked one.

Mercy
Go along! I don't know what I shall ever do if I have to see too much of you. I'll go.

Jonas
Hallo, don't go.

Mercy
Oh, you're very anxious I should stay, fright, ain't you?

Jonas
Yes, I am. I want to speak to you.

Mercy
Oh, do leave me alone, you monster, do.

Pecksniff
I'll just sit here by the fire with Mr. Chuffy.

(Jonas pulls Mercy and Charity beside him.)

Jonas
Now, both arms full.

Mercy
One will be black and blue if you don't let me go, you villain.

Jonas
Ah, I don't mind your pinching.

Mercy
Pinch him for me, Charity. I never did hate anyone as I hate this creature, I declare.

Jonas
No, no, don't say that. I want to be serious. I say, cousin Charity!

Charity (sharply)
Well! What?

Jonas
I want to prevent any mistakes and put everything upon a pleasant understanding. That's desirable and proper, ain't

it?

(Neither sister utters a sound.)

Jonas
Ahem. She'll not believe what I'm going to say, will she, cousin?

Charity
What are you going to say, Cousin?

Jonas
Why, you see. I know she'll laugh or pretend to. But you can tell her I'm in earnest cousin, can't you? (Pause). Nobody else can tell her what pains I took to get her into company. Nobody else can tell her how hard I tried to get to know you better in order to get to know her better. I always asked you about her. Where she had been, done, and so on. Didn't I, cousin? (silence) You'll be honest witness, won't you? You'll confirm it, every word. You must. Mercy, will you have me for your husband, eh?

(Charity runs out.)

Mercy
Let me go after her.

Jonas
Not till you say yes.

Mercy
No, I won't. I can't bear the sight of you. You are a fright. Besides I always thought you loved my sister best. We all thought so.

Jonas
But that ain't my fault.

Mercy
Yes, it was. You know it was.

Jonas
Any trick in love or war. You know. She may have thought I liked her best, but you didn't.

Mercy
I did.

Jonas
You never could have thought so when you were by.

Mercy
There's no accounting for tastes. I didn't mean to say that. I don't know what I mean. Let me go to her.

Jonas
Say yes, and then I will. I'll be very rich one day.

Mercy
If ever I brought myself to say so, it should only be that I might hate you and tease you all my life.

(She leaves during Jonas' speech.)

Jonas
That's as good as saying it outright. It's a deal. We're a pair if ever there was one.

Charity (returns)
Papa, take me home. This wretch has proposed to Mercy before my very face.

Pecksniff
Who has what?

Charity
He has! That thing—Jonas.

Pecksniff
Indeed?

Charity
Is that all you can say?

Pecksniff
Charity, can you envy so your sister? Think of the seven deadly sins. Ah, envy, envy what a passion you are.

Charity
Am I to be driven mad? (runs out)

Pecksniff
Jonas, Jonas, the dearest wish of—

Jonas
Very well; I'm glad to hear it. Since this ain't the one you're so fond of you must come down with another thousand, you know. It's worth that to keep your treasure to yourself.

Pecksniff
Why, why, why—

Jonas
Is that my father snoring?

Pecksniff
I don't think so.

Jonas
Tread on his foot will you be so good? The foot next you is the gouty one.

Pecksniff
Err—

Jonas
He'll be out presently. I'll do it myself. I say, that's strange, he usually wakes—

Pecksniff
Is something wrong?

Jonas
I think he's dead. I used to joke, you know but I—I never wished him dead.

Pecksniff
Life, ah, life, how quickly you pass.

Jonas
Long enough with him. I say, don't go. Someone might say it was my doing.

Pecksniff
Your doing!

Jonas
People say such things. Mrs. Gamp!

Pecksniff
Allow me to extend my condolences.

Jonas
Congratulations are more in order. (calling) Mrs. Gamp!

Mrs. Gamp (entering)
Here I am, sir.

Pecksniff
Someone will have to take care of Mr. Chuffy.

Chuffy
I loved him. He was very good to me.

Pecksniff
Come, come, Mr. Chuffy, this won't do. We all die one day, Mr. Chuffy. You mustn't really.

Chuffy
My old friend and master.

Pecksniff
Be a man, Mr. Chuffy. Upon my word, this is worse than a weakness. This is bad, selfish, wrong. He has a nearer relation than you. See how he bears himself.

Chuffy
His own son. His own son.

Jonas
Will you please put Mr. Chuffy to bed, Mrs. Gamp, and then take care of my father's beloved remains. (wipes a tear)

Mrs. Gamp
I hope I know what my dooty is. I have seen a deal of trouble my own self. I can feel for them as have their feelings tried but I am not a Rooshan or a Prooshan and consequently cannot suffer spies to be set over me. It is no easy matter to live when you are lift a wider-woman. Some people may be Rooshans and some may be Prooshans, they are born so and will please themselves. Them which is of other natures

thinks different.

Pecksniff
Mr. Chuffy is troublesome to her.

Jonas
Oh, very well, I'll take him out. Help me, will you, Pecksniff.

Pecksniff
Shall I say the sermon?

Jonas
Of course.

Pecksniff
It will cost $25.

Jonas
What's money?

Pecksniff
Jonas, you surprise me. (rehearsing) Dearly beloved, we are gathered here to witness the passing of brother Anthony. Who can say what Anthony was? But we can share in his experiences. He was a husband—a father...

Mrs. Gamp
Ah! Ah, dear! When Gamp was summoned and lying in Guy's Gospeal with a penny piece on each eye, and his wooden leg under his left arm, I thought I should have fainted away, but I bore up. It was hard but I saw it all through. Dedicated his body to science. That was hard. One's first way is to find such things a trial to the feelings. If it wasn't for the nerve a little sip of liquor gives me. I never was able to use more than a taste of it. I would never get through it. Mrs. Harris, I says, Mrs. Harris leave the bottle, leave the bottle on the chimney

piece and don't ask me to take more, but let me put my lips to it when I am so disposed. "Mrs. Gamp," she says, in answer "if ever there was a sober creature to be had for eighteen pence a day for working people and three and six for gentlefolks"—night watching being an extra charge "you are that invaluable person." "Mrs. Harris," I says, "If I could afford to do it for nothink I would, but I always say to them be they gents or ladys—is don't ask whether I won't take none or whether I will, but just leave the bottle on the chimney piece and let me put my lips to it when I am so disposed."

(Mrs. Gamp removes a bottle from somewhere on her person and half empties it at one swig.)

CURTAIN

ACT II
SCENE 3

Old Martin's bedroom in America.

(Pecksniff is sitting by Old Martin's bed. Old Martin lets a long spurt of tobacco juice into a distant spittoon.)

Pecksniff
I was afraid.

Old Martin
I can calc'late my distance, sir, to an inch. (Old Martin demonstrates) I require, sir, two foot clear in a circular direction and can engage myself to keep within it. I have gone ten feet, in a circ'lar direction but that was on a bet.

Pecksniff
Dear Old Martin. My dear Cousin.

Old Martin
Don't "dear old Martin" me. Do you see tickler? (pointing to his sword)? Do you see ripper? It ain't long since I shot a man for less. I like a duel. I was good in my day. I have seen a man less offensive than you made into sassafras juice—

Pecksniff
But, I came only with the best intentions. Your relatives—

Old Martin
What are they to me?

Pecksniff
Blood, sir, blood.

Old Martin
What have they ever done for me?

Pecksniff
Blood is thicker than water.

Old Martin
You may find the truth of that.

Pecksniff
In the name of the gentle shipherd whom you serve—

Old Martin
Are you a—in the name of Christ, will you get out and stop pestering me?

Pecksniff
Isn't the name of Jesus enough?

Old Martin
Go to hell!

Pecksniff
I come here only with the charity of Christ in my heart.

Old Martin
Go to hell, I say. And take your charity with you.

Pecksniff
You have wronged me, but I forgive you. I shall go. I will pray

for you.

Old Martin
And when you get there, stay there! At least until you're well done.

Doctor
I think, sir, you had better not excite him. Now, I had a similar case—

(Pecksniff goes out with Doctor. Doctor reenters.)

Old Martin
Has he gone at last?

Doctor
I told him you'd be in a better mood tomorrow. He'll be back. Cigarette, eh?

Old Martin
No. Light me a cigar.

Doctor
There you are.

Old Martin
And, I think a whisky will be necessary. Enduring that man is more than I can bear at times. I've never met anyone, no, not anyone more immoral.

Doctor
A twist of lemon, eh?

(Old Martin rises from the bed and throws off his invalid's disguise. He puts on a handsome dressing gown and reveals a vigorous man of his late sixties. He is far from death's door.)

Old Martin
Yes, thank you, Jobling.

Doctor
Very welcome, Martin. Do you think he'll come back again? This is the third time you've sent him away.

Old Martin
That just whets his appetite. He can smell money. The hungrier he gets, the more he drools.

Doctor
I can hardly understand why you go to such trouble to fleece Pecksniff. There are others easier to be had.

Old Martin
Doctor, I have fleeced many men in my day, but none so deserving. As you get older, you feel the need to do a good deed. To justify your existence. Gulling Pecksniff is my gift to humanity.

Doctor
But, why Pecksniff? There are others.

Old Martin
Because I hate him. I hate all my family; I want vengeance. I made my fortune in the slave trade. I was poor once. And those hypocrites, until I was definitely established, they wouldn't look at me. Once I'd made good—by selling human flesh—they forgot the past, conveniently, in the hopes I'd remember 'em in my will. Well, I've remembered 'em, but not in my will. Send in this fellow Tigg.

(Doctor goes to another door and returns with Montague Tigg.)

Montague

Evenin', gents both. You will understand that I am the accredited agent of your nephew Chevy Slyme. I am the ambassador from the court of Slyme.

Old Martin

Slyme—my dear old nephew, Chiv?

Montague

The same. There is, at this present moment, in this very place, a perfect constellation of talent, of genius, who is involved, though in what I cannot designate because of the culpable negligence of my friend Pecksniff, in a situation, as tremendous, perhaps, as the social intercourse of the nineteenth century will readily admit of.

Old Martin

My, my. What seems to be the matter? You are a noble friend to my nephew. I'm glad he has a friend like you.

Montague

As for my part in the same, don't mention it. Don't compliment me, because I can't bear it. Now, Uncle Martin, can I call you that? Have the goodness to do the utmost for my friend Slyme. Who wants money sorely. He is detained for a bill in the local inn. Indeed, I have been followed. Hannibal Challop had the great politeness to follow me to this house and is now waiting to see me home again. And, for that act of attention, sir, I can tell you that Hannibal Challop had better suffocated in his infancy than been preserved to this time.

Old Martin

My poor nephew.

Montague

Was there ever such a spirit as is possessed by that extraordinary individual? Was there ever such a Roman as our friend Chiv, Uncle? Was there ever such a man with such a classical turn of thought, and of such a toga-like simplicity of nature? Might he not, gents, both, I ask, have sat upon a tripod in ancient times, and prophesied to a perfectly unlimited extent if previously supplied with gin and water at the public cost?

Old Martin
Now, do you know what I am going to do for my nephew, Jobling, do you?

Jobling
Charity, eh?

Old Martin
I am going to do—absolutely nothing.

Montague
Sir, you have not been impressed by my friend Slyme. I am grieved, but not surprised. It is my own opinion, though I am a rough, thoughtless man, I can honor, mind. I know that beggarly relatives are not well liked!

Old Martin
They are not, indeed.

Montague
So, I ask you, in my own name, for my crushed friend. I ask the loan of three crowns distinctly and without a blush. I ask it almost as a right. They will be returned in a week. I feel that you will blame me for that sordid stipulation. Upon my soul, you mustn't make it more, not a trifle, indeed!

Old Martin
You amaze me, Mr. Tigg. I shall give you nothing to take to that wastrel. However, I will make your fortune if you will break

with that reprobate.

Montague
Stop, hold. There is a most remarkably long-headed, flowing-bearded and patriarchal proverb which observes that is the duty of man to be just before he is generous.

Old Martin
Jobling, this fellow is marvelous.

Jobling
A smasher—eh?

Old Martin
Jobling, let's make a gentleman of him. Quick, take off that stuff, Tigg. (Montague strips quickly) Now, Tigg, you are the ideal fellow. You have utterly no principles and you talk—why you can out—talk Pecksniff. You are the confidence man personified. With you I shall revenge myself on my relatives and mankind in general.

Montague
I always try to aid my friends.

Jobling
We are quite ready.

Old Martin
Pants.

Jobling
Striped, eh? Do they fit?

Old Martin
Shirt.

Jobling

Do you know I was called upon to attend a case somewhat curious. Tie, eh!

Montague

Well, I must say.

Old Martin

Hold still.

Jobling

Boots, eh? At about half past one I was called upon to attend that case. Hat and gloves, eh? Don't tie the tie too tight. That'll do. Cloak, eh?

Montague

Upon my unsullied word of honor—

Old Martin

Ah, Jobling, we couldn't have done better.

Jobling

He is a natural.

Montague

I must thank you for your beneficence and inquire what I must do to retain it. Assure yourself I will do nothing to stain the Tigg escutcheon.

Old Martin

To be sure of that we shall ask you to change your name from M. Tigg to T. G. Montague.

Montague

Well that comports well with my heritage. What must I do? Whose throat? (makes a motion of cutting a throat)

Old Martin
Nothing so drastic. Just pretend to be a wealthy British insurance broker.

Montague
I shan't have to lie? I can't bear a lie.

Old Martin
No. Just omit a few salient details. Now, Tigg, as you can see I am wealthy. But I love society no better for that. I made my money in the slave trade. I have side investments in various activities. I sell land in the Everglades. I reserve it for the aristocrats of nature. I get a very good price for it. I like to do my fellow creatures any service I can. The only trouble is few ever find it and of those who do few ever return to tell of it.

Montague
Feel my hands, sir? Are they clean?

Old Martin
Most remarkably dirty.

Montague
That is the point. Now I want them to be clean. Like yours. Manicured! To do that I have to dirty myself. My soul. Well so be it. But what do you need me for?

Old Martin
One dodge is never enough. I love money. I could make it honestly if I chose. I choose not to. I hate people. I want them to suffer. Now of all people, I hate my relatives most. Therefore, dear Montague—I need you. You shall have money, wealth, position—just like that.

Servant
Colonel Diver and Mr. Brick.

Old Martin
Ah, the very people. Diver, Brick, Mr. Montague, an insurance promoter from England.

Diver (entering with Brick)
Welcome to America!

Brick
To the palladium of national liberty.

Old Martin
Diver is the editor of the *New York Sewer*.

Diver
The organ of the local aristocracy.

Montague
Is that "organ" a pun? Aristocracy in America?

Diver
Of intelligence, sir. Intelligence. We make a discrimination of birth here. Only intelligence and money. Mr. Brick is our European correspondent. The aristocratic circles of your country quail before his name. (Brick huffs) You can tell us which of his articles is considered the most obnoxious.

Montague
It would be a difficult choice.

Brick
Let me ask you, sir, how do you like my country?

Montague
Well, I'm hardly prepared to say on such short notice.

Brick
Well, I should say you were not prepared for such signs of national prosperity. You have brought, I see, the usual amount of ignorance, poverty, and misery to this great palladium of national liberty—

Diver
I should not be surprised to hear you say you dislike my country. It requires an elevation and a preparation of the intellect. Your mind must be prepared for freedom.

Montague
I may say, sir—

Brick
European, quite European.

Diver
No dungeons here.

Montague
But—

Brick
European! Quite European.

Diver
No imports.

Montague
But—

Brick
European. Quite European.

Diver
No liveried servants here.

Montague
Err—

Brick
European, quite European.

Diver
You are not now in a despotic land. We are a model of the earth. No toadies here. We are the terrors of the British lion.

Brick
The British oppressors oppress not us.

Diver
The exclusiveness, the form, the ceremony, the artificial barriers set up between man and man, the division of the human race into court card and plain cards—anything but hearts—you do not witness that here—

Montague
Gentlemen.

Brick
European, quite European.

Diver
We are a new country, sir, we have not the excuse of having lapsed in the slow course of time into degenerate practices. We have no false gods; man, sir, here, is man in all his dignity.

Montague
But.

Brick
You are wrong, sir. But we will not pursue the subject, lest it should make you prejudiced. You have much to learn.

Old Martin
Mr. Montague, gentlemen, is a lord. Lord—(chuckling)

Diver
A lord? A real live spanker?

Old Martin
Genuine. One of England's oldest and richest.

Brick
Your Grace.

Diver
My Lord.

Brick
No, I'm first. Wait your turn.

Diver
Let me, I say. (shoving him aside) May I kiss your ring, Your Holiness?

Montague
Are they making fun of me?

Brick
I make this obeisance. You don't kiss his ring, you fool. Just watch me—do everything that I do. Your Grace, I kiss your—foot.

Montague
Gentlemen, you overwhelm me.

Diver
If we offended in any way—

Brick
If you desire any little service. If your boots need blacking.

Diver
May I help you to a wench?

Montague
I have seldom been received with such enthusiasm even in my own land.

Diver
Oh, we know how to treat a lord. Would Your Majesty—?

Old Martin
Gentlemen, gentlemen, you'll tire his lordship. You see, Montague, as a business man it is necessary that I have good press relations therefore I purchased the New York Sewer. Quietly, of course. Col. Diver is our editor-in-chief. Mr. Brick, one of the most remarkable young journalists in the country.

Montague
But you, you, my friend, are the master.

Brick
Oh, don't say that. It is never used in our country. We have abolished such trumpery distinctions. Everything has been resolved in favor of rationality.

Montague
There are only owners?

Old Martin
Precisely!

Montague
And the public.

Old Martin
Why, the public is very independent, just like the press.

Montague
But it allows itself to be *instructed*?

Diver
The free press—it is one of our ennobling institutions.

Old Martin
As slavery itself.

Brick
Hear, hear.

Old Martin
Now what you gentlemen may do for Lord T. G. Montague, Lord of Conbatten, is just this: print an article about our nation's distinguished guest; you will take mention my lord's connections, his estate, his vast holdings and his interest in forming the Anglo-American Disinterested Insurance and Loan Company. Now get the presses ready. We will have all the information you will require in a half hour. Well, what are you waiting for?

Brick
We haven't his lordship's permission to withdraw.

Diver
We can't stir, sir.

Brick
Your Grace, I am young and ardent. I aspirate for fame. It is my yearning and my thirst. Are you aware of any member of Parliament in England who would undertake to pay my expenses in that country for six months after my arrival? There is something within me which gives me the assurance that this enlightened patronage would not be thrown away. In literature or art, the bar, the pulpit or the stage: in one or the other I feel certain that I am to succeed.

Montague (beneficently)
I think I know one who might be willing to help you, young man.

Brick
Your lordship, I am a poet. There is poetry in wildness—every alligator basking in the sun is himself an epic. I shall write an ode to you.

Montague
Oh, do not, do not. You may withdraw.

(They do, humbly scraping all the way out.)

Old Martin
Did you ever see anything so ridiculous?

Montague
I thought they were satirizing me at first. Well, surely I must do something for poor Brick. I shall let him stay on my estate in Lincolnshire at no cost.

Old Martin
Why, that is generous of you.

Montague
Well, what now?

Old Martin
Now we must get you properly dressed and housed and equipped. All in the course of a day. Tomorrow you are coming out.

(Montague at window.)

Montague
I say, who is that pretty young filly headed up the walk?

Old Martin
Ah that must be Miss Pecksniff.

Montague
She may recognize me.

Old Martin
You were acquainted?

Montague
Only on one occasion.

Old Martin
She'll never know you. I'd better get into bed.

Servant
Miss Pecksniff.

(Mercy enters.)

Mercy
Oh, my dear uncle.

Old Martin
Is it my niece?

Mercy
It is, dear uncle. Your only niece.

Old Martin
Why that's very nice, niece.

Montague
I say, Martin, aren't you going to be polite?

Old Martin
Of course. Miss Pecksniff—Mr. Montague, Lord Conbatten. Lord Conbatten—my niece.

Mercy
Hello.

Montague
Hallo.

Mercy
You seem very familiar.

Montague
I have that kind of face. You see familiar to me, too.

Mercy
I have that kind of face. Don't you think it's fate?

Montague
It might be. When can I see you?

Mercy
You will always be welcome.

Old Martin
I say, is it polite to whisper?

Mercy
Sorry, uncle, Mr. Montague and I just realized we had met once before.

Old Martin
Oh—that's 'im—where?

Montague
At a ball I gave in London once. Isn't that it?

Mercy
Yes.

Old Martin
Would you be so kind, Lord Conbatten. to step to Colonel Diver's office and take care of that business.

Montague
I should be happy, sir. Young lady.

Mercy
My lord.

(Montague goes.)

Mercy
Ain't he handsome, uncle?

Old Martin
Can't say I noticed that.

Mercy
He's a fine figure of a man.

Old Martin
Is he though?

Mercy (changing her tactics)
Not as handsome as you, though.

Old Martin
You really thinks so?

Mercy
Would I lie?

Old Martin
Did your father send you here?

Mercy
Pa wouldn't do such a thing.

Old Martin (ironic)
Your father's so concerned about my health.

Mercy
He's even brought you two wonderful nurses from London to care for you, uncle, at his own expense: Mrs. Gamp and Mrs. Prig.

(Mrs. Gamp and Mrs. Prig enter nervously, smiling and curtysing)

Old Martin (aghast)
Very kind of him, I'm sure. (aside, to himself) Does he really plan to kill me? (aloud) Thanks, but I have a horror of nurses.

Mercy
But, uncle.

Old Martin
But me no buts. No, I say!

Mercy (sighing)
As you wish. (she gestures, and the nurses leave. Martin utters a sigh of relief.

Old Martin (aside)
Those two would stop the Messiah from coming. (to himself) Those two really give me the shivers. Let's change the subject. I hear you're going to marry Jonas?

Mercy
I'm engaged to him.

Old Martin
Do you love him?

Mercy
Love him. I hate him. The fright.

Old Martin
You're not being forced into this?

Mercy
No.

Old Martin
Do you want to break the engagement?

Mercy
I've never given it a thought.

Old Martin
Wouldn't you rather stay here and take care of me? Tell Jonas to go fly a kite.

Mercy
Are you asking me to be your nurse?

Old Martin
No.

Mercy
La, sir. You aren't proposing?

Old Martin
No, I ain't proposing. I'm making a proposition.

Mercy
You mean you're asking me to be your mistress? Why, you old fright. I'd prefer Jonas to that.

Old Martin
Heir to a 100 million when I die. If you don't want a permanent position I can give you a high retainer for one night.

Mercy
No, I can't. Not any more. And I'm not going to marry Jonas either. (starts to run out)

Old Martin
Now don't take on like that. I was just testing you. You tell your Pa I want to see him and tell him what a daughter he has got. Now, dear, come kiss your uncle.

BLACKOUT/CURTAIN

Pecksniff (entering)
I have come back hoping to find you in a more receptive mood, sir.

Old Martin
Pecksniff I have made no secret of the fact I distrusted you.

Pecksniff
No—you have not.

Old Martin
And I still do.

Pecksniff
Ah, sir, how the meek and unoffending are maligned. Had I been what you think me, Art would have taught me how to insinuate myself into your good graces. But as I am honest I have no defenses—

Old Martin
Well, submit to a test?

Pecksniff
In any way I can.

Old Martin
Mercy, would you go in the other room, I need to speak to your father privately.

(she nods and goes out)

Sir, put a case. Had you a child, or someone dear to you who did an immoral thing; a thing you could not approve, would you be just?

Pecksniff
I should try. I hope that I would be merciful.

Old Martin
Now then suppose the crime deserved no mercy.

Pecksniff
I do not wish to be a judge.

Old Martin
At some point, Pecksniff we must judge it is unavoidable if we believe in anything at all.

Pecksniff
You reason persuasively, but to what purpose?

Old Martin
Now suppose you had a child, a daughter.

Pecksniff
Oh, I do. Two, in fact. Angels.

Old Martin
And say one were your favorite.

Pecksniff
And I have a favorite.

Old Martin
And say this favorite betrayed you.

Pecksniff
But dear little Mercy would never—why, she isn't clever—

Old Martin
Say this favorite child came to see an old man on his death bed

almost and offered herself to him so that she might be his widow—or at least a well rewarded—err, "housekeeper" is I believe the more decorous phrase. Say that your daughter Mercy were this girl—what then?

Pecksniff
Sir, you have said enough. How you have wounded my heart. To think that I have cherished a viper there. Oh, better it were that she had killed me. The pain of knowing this. It is too much, too much. I am nearly overcome. To cheat me. Her own Pa. Enough, enough.

Old Martin
What will you do?

Pecksniff
Let us say I have a duty to discharge to society. Excuse me, sir,—excuse me. Mercy, you can come in now.

Old Martin
Jolly.

Mercy
Is everything settled, Pa?

Pecksniff
Yes, things are settled.

Mercy
And is our dear cousin pleased?

Pecksniff
He will be. Are you well, my dear?

Mercy
Yes very well, Pa.

Pecksniff
Very good, very good. I am glad to hear it. You were well treated as a child were you not?

Mercy
Why of course, Pa. But why are you asking me such strange questions?

Pecksniff
And I always gave way to your wishes didn't I?

Mercy
Yes, but—?

Pecksniff
And you were brought up to be a Christian, were you not? I did not fail in that, I hope.

Mercy
Of course not, Pa. I'm a good Methodist, just like you. Pa, you alarm me.

Pecksniff
Oh, Mercy, Mercy, I wonder you can look me in the face.

Mercy
But what on earth?

Pecksniff
I will not dwell upon the past. I will spare you and myself that pain at least.

Mercy
I'm glad you won't do that, but will you please explain—the present—??

Pecksniff
The *present* is enough, and the sooner *that* is past, the better. I will not dismiss you without an explanation, though such a course would be justified. It might wear the appearance of hurry and I will not do it for I am perfectly self-possessed.

Mercy
But, Pa, I don't understand.

Pecksniff
Stop. I know what you will say. But it won't do. All is known. (looks significantly)

Mercy
But, Pa.

Pecksniff
Please don't add perjury to your crime.

Mercy
What crime?

Pecksniff
I know you will try to justify yourself.

Mercy
But, Pa.

Pecksniff
You may even lie.

Mercy
Pa!

Pecksniff
Silence. Here, count this money. It is yours. My last gift. Take

it, and go. Leave my house. Make your living as the harlot that you are. I disown you. Oh mendacity, mendacity. what a sin you are! I will not say what a blow this is. I will not say how it tries me; how it works upon my nature, how it grates my feelings.

Old Martin
Pecksniff. I say—

Pecksniff
I do not care for that.

Old Martin
But, isn't this really a little harsh?

Pecksniff
I can endure as well as another man, but I hope—

Old Martin
Really, Pecksniff—

Pecksniff
I hope that this mendacity of yours may not alter my ideas of humanity.

Mercy
Pa.

Pecksniff
That it may not impair my freshness.

Mercy
Pa. Please, I don't understand.

Pecksniff
Or contract, if I may use the expression, my opinions.

Mercy
Pa!

Old Martin
Pecksniff!

Pecksniff
I hope it will not, I don't think it will. It may be a comfort to you to know that I shall endeavor not to think the worse of my fellow creatures, for what has passed between us. We part and are strangers from this time.

Old Martin
Pecksniff, do nothing in haste.

Pecksniff
I have a duty to society, sir, and it shall be discharged at any cost. Oh, is it not enough that these blows fall on me but must they also hit my friends.

Mercy
Father!

Pecksniff
If a fiery serpent had proclaimed it from the top of Salisbury Cathedral, I would have said—"That serpent lied."

Mercy
Mr. Chuzzlewit, help me.

Pecksniff
No, young woman. None of that. Strike here, mistress, here. Launch your arrows at me not at him.

Mercy
Oh Mr. Chuzzlewit, he's gone mad. Help me. I implore you,

hear me speak.

Pecksniff

Would you accost venerable virtue? Would you? Know that it is not defenseless. I will be its shield, young woman.

Old Martin

Calm yourself, Pecksniff.

Pecksniff

I can't be calm. Is there no refuge for you?

Old Martin

Stand aside and let me see her.

Pecksniff

It is right that you should see her. Behold. There she is. There she is. The Scarlet woman.

Old Martin

Say what you wish to say.

Pecksniff

His sense of justice is so fine, that he will even listen to her. Ingenuous mind.

Mercy

I don't know what has come over Pa. I certainly don't deserve this. Help me. Someone has traduced me to him.

Pecksniff

Did you speak worthy, sir? I know what you thought. Let her go on. The development of self-interest in the human mind is always a curious study. Let her go on, sir?

Mercy

Someone has lied to him. I don't understand. Can't you make him explain? I can clear myself I am sure, if he will only explain? I will make whoever said it tell the truth.

Pecksniff

Beautiful truth. How is your name profaned, by false mankind. It is hard to bear with mankind, dear sir, but let us do so meekly. It is only our duty. I know what you are thinking of but don't express it prematurely. Do not give way to this. It is very natural. But you must not allow shameless conduct to move you. Think of me, my friend.

Old Martin

You recall me to myself.

Pecksniff

Indignation will bring the scalding tear to the honest eye, but we have higher duties to perform than that. Shall I give expression to your thoughts, my friend?

Old Martin

Yes. Speak for me.

Pecksniff

Young woman, the door is immediately behind you. Blush if you can. Begone without a blush if you can't.

Mercy

Father, what have I done?

Pecksniff

Do not suppose the tear in my eye is shed for you. Oh, no. It is shed for him. It is shed for him. And for myself. For him whom you seek to make the victim of your arts. You shall not wrong him further with your indecent proposals whilst I have life. You must strike at him through me. And you will find me an ugly customer.

Mercy
Ah, now I understand. You're responsible for this. You old skinflint. You—

Old Martin
You have nothing more to say. Tell her, Pecksniff, she has not the decency to be contrite.

Pecksniff
You have heard him. It is all over. Go. Get out. Leave my house. Be gone before I return. Or rather don't go home. You may send for your clothes.

Mercy
I'll be even with <u>you</u> and <u>you</u>. (runs out)

Old Martin
Well, Pecksniff, I didn't believe you were such a man. You excite my admiration. I own I couldn't have treated my daughter so—low. Jolly.

Pecksniff
I am relieved it's over. It was a duty I had to discharge to society.

Old Martin
Go after her. I wish to have a word with her privately. Oh, by the way, I'm going to put myself entirely in your hands. You'll be my secretary. Everything—but go after her.

Pecksniff
Do you trust yourself?

Old Martin
My heart will not relent.

(Pecksniff goes and soon Mercy enters.)

Mercy
You did this to me!

Old Martin
That I did, Ducky, and I did it pretty well didn't I? Done up.

Mercy
Why?

Old Martin
Revenge. But, more than that—to put you in a position where you can't refuse me.

Mercy
Do you think I can be bought?

Old Martin
I do indeed. And by the way since you rejected my first offer I don't plan to make the next offer so attractive by half.

Mercy
If I refused that, why should I accept a worse—

Old Martin
Why, because you need money, darling. Jonas won't marry you now. How will you support yourself? You're too well-bred to be honest. Therefore it follows you must take the easiest way.

Mercy
If I ever do, it won't be with you.

Old Martin
Oh, skittish. Will you never learn? Fa, la, I can wait. When you're starving you won't be so choosey. I can wait.

Mercy
I'm too proud.

Old Martin
And besides, I'm not as unattractive as the others you may have to serve. (runs to the door and locks it, withdrawing the key) Now, shall we have a quiet talk?

Mercy
Who do you think you are? Do you know who I am?

Old Martin
Perfectly, dear girl. You are the penniless Miss Mercy Pecksniff and I am the rich, respected and honored sadist, Martin Chuzzlewit, at your service.

Mercy
I am a minister's daughter. Have you no respect for the cloth?

Old Martin
Why, enough to dishonor it only on a special occasion unlike your father who dishonors it every day of his life. Now, dear girl, before I let you leave this room I intend to hear you talk like the reasonable woman nature made you. Now, don't flounce about, you'll only muss your clothes.

Mercy
There are men of honor to avenge—

Old Martin
You've used your lovers too meanly to expect anything but ridicule. And do you expect cousin Jonas to extend himself

in gallantry. Dear girl, be reasonable. If you were a fool I wouldn't seek to make you see reason.

Mercy
Let go of me.

Old Martin
Come, come. A word or two will establish a pleasant understanding between us. I am not angry, dear girl.

(She runs about.)

Mercy
You! Angry!

Old Martin
Look, behind you. Think—old age will over take you—wrinkles.

Mercy
That's a thought.

Old Martin
Why not yield to reason when you see it. Let's be jolly.

Mercy
Jolly, Mr. Chuzzlewit?

Old Martin
Say—Martin!

Mercy (softly)
Martin—you old fright. You're a greater horror than Jonas.

Old Martin
Now, that's slander. I like to be jolly sometimes. I ain't so sour as

I seem. My personality are not absolutely those of a monster, I trust. Ah, naughty hand why did you take me prisoner? So, go. (slaps it, then pets it and squeezes it) What do you say, let's be jolly?

Mercy
If you use your superior strength. I hate you, fright.

Old Martin
Oh no, no. Let's be jolly.

Mercy
Nothing seems to move you. Oh, fright. How can a monster be so good-natured?

Old Martin
Dear girl—'shabit of self-examination and the practice of—

Mercy
Lechery.

Old Martin
Jollity. Jollity calms my spirit to such a beatific degree that I am not easily—And did you think you could ruffle me? You will consent, dear girl. You will consent. Ah, such a little hand—shall I bite it?

Mercy
And if I did consent, fright, just how do you propose to be jolly?

Old Martin
Oh, I am very jolly. Kiss me, Mercy.

Mercy
Kiss me. Hang you, fright—

Old Martin

I love jollity, dearly. I'll kiss you for joking. And ruffle you for joking, ho, ho, ho—

Mercy

Ain't you a little old for this, fright? You should think of death at your age. It is more fitting to think of the grave, not on such vanities as kissing.

Old Martin

Death, my little Mercy. How jolly, dear girl. Some twenty years hence, perhaps. But even if I were on my last leg. When better to think of such vanities—before it is too late.

Mercy

You good-for-nothing—except to pay expenses—

Old Martin

And what is more important than that? Now let's sit down.

Mercy

Oh, you sit, fright; I'm sure your legs are weak, I'm fine as I am.

Old Martin

Why, I'm as strong as a goat and I can butt. Baa—baa—(charges at her, head lowered, making horns)

Mercy

Please be a little more domestic, old goat.

Old Martin

Why, then I shall be a cat and catch my mistress' skirts. (catches her skirt and pulls it up) Purr, pretty lady, purr.

Mercy
Fright, put my skirts down.

Old Martin
Will you be reasonable? There's plenty of money to be had from me.

Mercy
How much?

Old Martin
Why, you can name your price.

Mercy
In that case, Martin, I'll agree, but only to torment you as much as I can.

Old Martin
Jolly. (smiles)

BLACKOUT/CURTAIN

ACT II
SCENE 4

The lavishly furnished Board Room of the Anglo-American Disinterested Life Insurance Company.

A room.

Jobling
Old Martin is very pleased.

Montague
He has reason.

Jobling
This swindle is the most successful since the Yazoo lands of fond memory. Ah, those were the days.

Montague
It will be more successful.

Jobling
It only remains to hook Jonas Chuzzlewit and Pecksniff. This idea is, I may say, an *idée fixe* with Martin. Unless he catches those flies all the rest will be a disappointment.

Bellamy (entering)
Sir. Mr. Jonas Chuzzlewit.

Montague
Speak of the Devil.

Jobling
A very apt phrase. Positively you know—that's ha ha—epigrammatic. I invited him.

Montague (to Jonas, who enters)
Ah, my dear sir. I *am* delighted. Jobling, you know, I believe.

Jobling
I think so. I trust I have that honor. I hope so. I see you well, my dear sir. Quite well. That's well.

Montague
A glass of wine?

Jonas
No. No. Not over business. All very well for you though.

Montague
What an old hand you are, Mr. Jonas.

Jobling
I'll just step out while you two do business. I can be found in the medical room.

Jonas
Not such an old hand, neither. I'm getting married. Green of me, you'll say. But she has a good dower. But then, no one ever knows what may happen to these women. I'm thinking—of insuring her life. It's but fair a man should have some consolation.

Montague
Yes—consolation.

Jonas
But I'd like to do it without bothering her about it. She might take it in her head that her days are numbered.

Montague
Sweet, silly simpleton.

Jonas
And because the insurance company I did business with before was rather—well they asked too many snooping questions. Now the truth is—

Montague
Pleas don't use that Sunday school expression.

Jonas
What's the security?

Montague
Why, the paid up capital.

Jonas
Oh! I understand all about paid up capital.

Montague
You do?

Jonas
I should hope so.

Montague
I know you do, I know you do. Look at me. You recalled the—phiz?

Jonas
No. Not exactly.

Montague
Pecksniff's parlor at Todgers. I'm Montague Tigg. Do you find me at all changed?

Jonas
By god. Rather.

Montague
I was perhaps a bit ill kempt.

Jonas
Precious seedy.

Montague
Do you see that carriage? Do you know whose it is? Mine. Do you like this room?

Jonas
It must have cost a lot of money.

Montague
Mine, too. Why don't you take premiums instead of paying 'em. Join us.

Jonas
You ain't a bad man of business. You know how to set about it. I will say.

Montague
Tut, tut, Mr. Chuzzlewit, we are grown men, I hope. You see that crowded street. There are printed calculations, which will tell you pretty nearly how many people will pass up and down in the course of a day. I can tell you how many of 'em will come in here. Merely, because we are here. Join us, you shall come in cheap. We are a collection agency. Another man, I shouldn't have told, but you are too deep for us. Dine

with me tomorrow.

Jonas
I will.

Montague
Done. Wait a bit. Peruse this document. I am the surety on the company. I am the only responsible person in the company. Security: my vast English estates.

Jonas
But what happens if you have a couple of unlucky deaths?

Montague
Why, we did. I had to mortgage almost everything until I realized—

Jonas
Realized, realized what?

Montague
Why, to investigate. We're still investigating.

Jonas
But one fine day they'll all die.

Montague
True. Then there is but one thing to do.

Jonas
Why, you're as bold as brass.

Montague
Now, Jonas, I make you a proposition. You came to America to get old Chuzzlewit's money didn't you?

Jonas
Who told you that?

Montague
A little bird. Now, Jonas, you realize that Pecksniff is a bit beforehand with you. He is now Old Martin's secretary.

Jonas
The Devil he is.

Montague
You won't stand a chance of getting to—

Jonas
Old Chuzzlewit with Pecksniff around.

Montague
You know how Pecksniff will outmaneuver you.

Jonas
That's true enough.

Montague
Therefore, you must reach Chuzzlewit's money through Pecksniff.

Jonas
How?

Montague
First, we must persuade Pecksniff this is a good investment. Get him to invest his own money. Then by degrees we persuade him—to embezzle Chuzzlewit's money! Do you like the idea?

Jonas
Very much!

Montague
And when we get it?

Jonas
We bolt!

Montague
You'll dine with me tomorrow?

Jonas
At what time?

Montague
Seven. Take the documents. I see your answer. Tomorrow we'll arrange the details.

Jonas
There's a good deal to be looked into first.

Montague
You shall look into anything you please. But wait a bit. Let's have lunch together now.

Jonas
Well, that's an idea.

Montague
Surely you won't refuse a glass of wine and some refreshment?

Jonas
Well, on the condition we don't talk business I don't mind if I do.

Montague

Excellent. It will be duck *à la* pheasant *à* caviar. I'll invite, the board—I'm not sure. I think it best not to have a party, but—

Jonas

Why what do you call this? You don't mean to say you do this every day.

Montague

Why, whenever I dine with the board I expect several guests.

Jonas

Oh, well, in that case, I can't refuse.

Montague

This is my common style. I prefer not to be pretentious.

Jonas

Ecod, no.

Montague

I'm sure when you join us you'll dispose of your share of the profits in the same way.

Jonas

Well, no, I can't say that I will.

Montague

Well, no doubt, you're judicious but one of the company must do it for appearance alone. You don't mind dining expensively at another's expense do you?

Jonas

Ah. On the contrary.

Montague
Bellamy.

Bellamy
Sir.

Montague
Let the medical officer know with my compliments, that I wish to see him.

(Enter Jobling.)

Montague
Jobling, my dear friend, how are you? Bellamy, wait outside—don't leave us.

Jobling
And how are *you*, Mr. Montague, eh? How are you? A little worn with business, eh? If so rest. A little feverish from wine, humph. If so, water? Nothing at all the matter, and quite comfortable. Then take some lunch? I always take it myself about this time of day, you know.

Montague
Bellamy.

Bellamy
Sir.

Montague
Lunch.

Jobling
Not on my account, I hope. You are very good. Thank you. At any rate if you don't take lunch, you'll very soon come under my hands.

Montague
Anything to prevent that, Jobling.

Jobling
Allow me to illustrate with Mr. Jonas' leg. In this leg you will observe, here where the knee fits the socket—between the bone and the socket a certain quality of animal oil.

Jonas
Why do you pick my leg out? It's the same with other legs, ain't it?

Jobling
Never mind. That doesn't matter.

Jonas
But I do mind.

Jobling (unmoved)
In this portion of the leg, there is a certain amount of animal oil. In every one of Mr. Jonas' joints there is the same deposit. Very good. If he neglects to eat, the oil wanes. What is the consequence? Mr. Jonas' bones sink in their socket and Mr. Jonas becomes a wizened, puny, stunted miserable man! (lets the leg fall with a clump) Yes, we know a few of nature's secrets. We study for that. It is extraordinary how little is known on these subjects generally. Now where do you suppose Mr. Jonas' stomach is?

Jonas
Here.

Jobling
Not at all, not at all. Quite a popular mistake. Sir, you are altogether deceived.

Jonas
I feel it here.

Jobling
You think you do. I had a patient, now deceased, who left me a handsome legacy by the by, who was so over come by my telling him this that he became speechless and later died.

Bellamy
By your leave, there, by your leave. Refreshment for the boardroom. (enters)

Jobling
The true life insurance, Mr. Montague.

Montague
Commission to you doctor on four new policies and a loan. Jobling, long life to you.

Jobling
No, no. Upon my word I've no right to draw the commission. I haven't really, it's picking your pocket. I don't recommend anybody here. I only say what I know. If they ask me about capital resources, there I confess myself at fault. I have no head for figures. Do I know, Mr. Montague? Why of course, capital fellow. A remarkably handsome man and quite the gentleman in every respect. Property, I am told, in England. House and everything belonging to him, beautiful. Costly furniture on the most elegant and lavish scale. And pictures which even in an anatomical point of view are per-fection. Do they wish to know whether they are in good enough health to obtain insurance? Why, I will pass there. Fine shape. The truth and nothing else. Caution is my weak side. Whether I would repose confidence in this company if I had not been paying money elsewhere for many years—that's quite another question. I do my best to look as I would.

Montague
Doctor, you are incomparable. Bellamy!

Bellamy
Sir.

Montague
Clear. No I thought it best not to have a party. Let him take us in the rough, I said. And pretty smooth too, ecod. This doesn't cost a trifle. No. To be candid it does not. But I like this sort of thing. You're tolerably comfortable, I hope?

Jobling
Oh! You needn't trouble your head about me. Famous. Excellent. Men of the world, my dear sir. Thorough men of the world. To a professional person like myself, it's quite refreshing to come into this kind of society. It's not only agreeable—and nothing can be more agreeable or philosophically improving. It's character, my dear sir, character.

Jonas
Gentlemen, I must go.

Jobling
And, I too.

Montague
Bellamy.

Bellamy
Sir.

Montague
Show the gentlemen out, Bellamy!

Bellamy
Sir.

Montague
Call in Mr. Nadgett. (Nadgett enters) Nadgett, any information you can get me about Jonas Chuzzlewit I shall be glad to have. Never mend its character. Anything. And Nadgett. Bring it to *me*.

(Nadgett goes out. Mercy rushes in.)

Bellamy
See here, you can't just walk into the boardroom unannounced.

Montague
It's all right, Bellamy. Mr. Nadgett that will be all.

(Doors are closed.)

Mercy
My darling.

Montague
My angel. But you mustn't come here. It's too dangerous.

Mercy
Old Martin is not suspicious.

Montague
But you know that I am in his power—temporarily.

Mercy
Yes. And so am I?

Montague
You?

Mercy
He has made my father think that I tried to marry him. Father threw me out of the house.

Montague
Oh, the villains. Why, they both deserve all that I planned to do to them anyway. Heaven: how just you are.

Mercy
And he wants *me*, Montague.

Montague
Oh, no.

Mercy
He has offered me money. Or I should say promised it.

Montague
You refused.

Mercy
I am a rational creature.

Montague
You accepted.

Mercy
I had no choice.

Montague
Does honor mean nothing?

Mercy
Very little in matters of necessity.

Montague
And what about me?

Mercy
He will not be the first old man who will be deceived by his mistress. But I love you, darling.

Montague
You must put him off.

Mercy
What good will that do?

Montague
Oh, a great deal. A little time is all I need. He does not suspect us yet. Therefore, I can subsidize you for a few weeks. Hold out just for a short while.

Mercy
I suppose it will not be a bad idea at any rate. I'll keep him interested and that will whet his appetite, should I have to give up in the end.

Montague
Ah, what a clever thing you are.

Mercy
I must think for both of us. I'm the practical one.

Montague
I wouldn't want a girl who couldn't take care of herself and me, too.

Mercy
I wouldn't want a man who didn't appreciate such a girl.

Montague
We're a match.

BLACKOUT/CURTAIN

ACT II
SCENE 5

The Same, a few weeks later.

Montague
Well, Mr. Nadgett, any news?

Nadgett
I think so.

Montague
Good. I began to fear you were off the scent.

Nadgett
Scent is a strange thing. A strange thing. Sometimes you smell it, sometimes you don't. It depends partly on the thing smelled and partly on the—smeller. If I may coin an expression.

Montague
You are truth itself, Mr. Nadgett. Do you report a great success?

Nadgett
That depends on what you think of this.

Montague
Do you think it good?

Nadgett

Why, yes—I think it will do. Read these notes.

Montague

Can't you explain it to me in a few words?

Nadgett

Err, no. Never can tell who might be listening. Now here's number one. Take that one first. Always begin at the beginning. Now number two. Always progress by successors.

Montague

This Jonas is really quite the boy.

Nadgett

Never conclude anything until all the evidence is in. Number three, if you please, end at the *end*.

Montague (smiles)

Marvelous, truly marvelous. Nadgett. You are a wonderful man.

Nadgett

I think it's a pretty good case. In short, he's bagged.

Montague

You'll be well rewarded for this.

Nadgett

The reward's in the work, sir. It is my ambition to bring the art of detection to the perfection of a science.

Montague

Why, Nadgett, you are a Galileo in your profession. In time to come men will build a monument to you. I think I heard a double knock—will you put your head out the window and tell me whether there is anyone at the door.

Nadgett
It's Jonas C.

Montague
Marvelous—simply marvelous.

Nadgett
Shall I go?

Montague
Yes, wait a bit. Hold. Stay here. Don't leave us alone together.

Jonas (entering)
Don't you answer your doors no more?

Montague
Bellamy is off tonight and I didn't hear you. You're very welcome.

Jonas
Hello. Who's that. Why, no, it's the old ghost come back to haunt me. Make him go away.

Montague
That's only Mr. Nadgett.

Jonas
Well! He's not wanted here I suppose. He may go mayn't he?

Montague
Oh, he's a mere piece of furniture, like Mr. Chuffy. Let him stay, let him stay. He has been told not to lose sight of certain friends of ours. He understands his business.

Jonas
The resemblance to my father is very disconcerting. Of all the precious old dummies in appearance that I ever saw, he's about the worst I think, save one. He's afraid of me, I think.

Montague
It's my belief you are poison to him. Nadgett! Give me that towel. You see my dear fellow—what's the matter with your lips. How white they are.

Jonas (rubbing his lips)
Vinegar. Oysters for breakfast. I don't believe they are white.

Montague
Now, I look again they are not. They are coming right again.

Jonas
Say, what you were going to say and let my face be. As long as I can show my teeth when I want to, the color of my lips is not material. See. (shows his teeth savagely)

Montague
Quite true. I was only going to say you are too quick and active for our friend. He is too shy to cope with you, but does his duty well.

Jonas
Bother him and his duty. I want a word with you. I am not satisfied with the state of affairs.

Montague
Dissatisfied? The money is pouring in.

Jonas
It pours in well enough but it don't pour out well enough. It's all in your hands. Ecod, what with one of your bylaws and

another of your bylaws and your votes in this capacity and your votes in that capacity and official rights and your individual rights and other peoples rights who are only you again, there are no rights left for me. I'm not going to stand for it, you know.

Montague
No.

Jonas
No.

Montague
I give you my honor—

Jonas
Damn your honor. You can have all the honor you like. All I want is a little more control over the money.

Montague
I supply the brains.

Jonas
Oh, you do, eh?

Montague
It's unfortunate I find you in this humor for I was about to propose to you for your advantage—solely for you advantage, that you should venture a little more with us.

Jonas
Was you, by God?

Montague
We should be delighted to receive your funds.

Jonas
How kind of you. You'd be delighted to receive 'em, would you?

Montague
I give you my sacred honor, quite transported.

Jonas
No doubt.

Montague
And very much to your advantage.

Jonas
Can you tell me how?

Montague
Delighted. *Shall* I?

Jonas
I think you had better. Strange things have been done in the insurance business before now. I mean to take care of myself.

Montague
Chuzzlewit! Strange things have been done and are done everyday and no one suspects them. But ours is a strange business and sometimes we find out about them.

Jonas
I think I'll sit down.

Montague
You'll not object to venture with us, my friend?

Jonas
No. (strangled)

Montague
Well, said that's like yourself.

Jonas
What would you have me do? What do you expect?

Montague
Confidence my good fellow. Some confidence. (injured tone)

Jonas
Ecod. You show great confidence in me. Don't you?

Montague
Now, Chuzzlewit, (very softly) notwithstanding what has passed I will be plain with you. Are you attending to me there! I only see your back. (fiercely) You are a little out of sorts, but I can make allowances for that. And am fortunately myself in the very best of tempers. Now let us see how circumstances stand. A few days ago I discovered—

Jonas
Don't. I, I—

Montague
Perhaps, there is something in it, perhaps, nothing but we don't even want it looked into, do we? No, I thought we didn't. However I should never think of using it against you.

Jonas
Using it to make a beggar of me. Is that the use you mean?

Montague
I wish you to venture a little more with us, that's all.

Jonas
How much?

Montague
Oh say, everything?

Jonas
You're crazy. I won't do it.

Montague
If you don't, my secret is worthless to me. Why keep a secret if it is worthless? I disown such a secret. Let the public care for it.

Jonas
I'm sure. I don't care for it at all. But I dare say, true or not, I'm no worse than other men.

Montague
Not a bit.

Jonas
Is it known to anyone else?

Montague
Only you.

Jonas
Ah, well, I'm yours. Wait, what about Nadgett?

Montague
He knows absolutely nothing. Would I confide in him? (A knock. Jonas jumps.) Who's that?

Montague
Ah—come in?

(Enter Pecksniff and Dr. Jobling. Nadgett opens the door and at a sign from Montague he goes out.)

Jobling
Ah, dear Mr. Montague. Chuzzlewit? Up late, eh? Dear Mr. Montague, this is Mr. Pecksniff. I treated him for a slight indisposition yesterday and just mentioned you in passing. Mr. Pecksniff asked to be introduced.

Montague
Ah, delighted, Mr. Pecksniff. I couldn't have been more pleasantly surprised.

Pecksniff
It is always well for a man of the cloth to look into the various philanthropic ventures started by private enterprise. We, in the clergy, encourage it, sir, we encourage it.

Montague
To be sure.

Jobling
Jonas, are you ill? You look rather bilious. Mr. Pecksniff, your nephew, I believe. Ah, yes indeed.

Pecksniff
My son-in-law, rather, that was to be.

Jonas
Still is. If I can't marry "the other one" I'll marry the other one. Same terms.

Jobling
Has something gone wrong?

Pecksniff
I am disappointed in one of my children, sir. It seems I nourished a viper—an adventuress. I threw her out.

Montague
That's heroic nowadays. You deserve a reward for that.

Jobling
Jonas, you do look ill. And you are bound for all our sakes to take particular care of your digestion, my dear sir. Depend upon it, it is worth preserving. It must be in admirable condition, perfect chronometer work. Otherwise your spirits could not be so remarkable. Your bosom sits lightly on the throne as what's his name says in his play. I wish he said it in a play which did anything like common justice to the medical profession, by the by. There is an apothecary in that drama sir which is a low thing, vulgar, sir, out of nature altogether.

(Jonas putters about. He opens Jobling's bag.)

Jonas
These your tools?

Jobling
Yes, indeed.

Jonas
Sharp, ain't they?

Jobling
Scalpels

Jonas
Remarkable.

Montague

Very remarkable. But, Mr. Pecksniff, I've surely kept you waiting?

Pecksniff

Oh, no. I'm quite content. I just heard a little bit about the company and thought I'd like to know a little bit more.

Montague

Perhaps, Jonas can tell you. He's our chief stockholder.

Pecksniff

Are you indeed? I respect your judgment, Jonas. Is the company's credit sound?

Jonas

Credit? Sound? Why you could borrow enough to put you well off for life on the office furniture alone. We don't have to borrow, we loan. LOAN, Pecksniff, *loan*. I've made—never mind what I've made. You know me pretty well and I don't blab about such things. But ecod, I've made a trifle.

Pecksniff

I am not a diplomatical character. My heart is in my hand. My hand in someone else.

Jonas

Someone else's pocket! Old hypocrite. You would be close. I could put you in the way of doubling your money in a month. Doubling that again in no time. It wouldn't be bad to keep a chance like this in the family but you're such a deep one.

Pecksniff

What will Mr. Montague think? You run on so, Jonas.

Jonas
He don't want to make a deal. You're wasting your time listening to this old hypocrite. He's too smart, too close for his own good. Don't tell him about the release clause.

Pecksniff
Clause, what clause?

Montague
Why it's—

Jonas
Hush not a word. He ain't interested. He don't care to hear it.

Pecksniff
But I do. I do.

Montague
And then there's the capital investment.

Pecksniff
Yes, yes.

Jonas
I tell you, he ain't interested.

Pecksniff
Don't listen to him at all.

Montague
Well as for the exculpatory clause reads "Whereas this, whereas that, whereas the other and provided that and so forth, the aforesaid—and the party of the first part and the party of the second part—that we aren't liable if the insured dies a natural death and after a few more whereas, wherefore, aforesaids—etc.—it turns out we aren't liable if the insured

did not die a natural death either.

Pecksniff
Then you have no liabilities.

Montague
Precisely.

Pecksniff
But this is genius. Is it legal?

Montague
By the time anyone figures out that it isn't, if it isn't—that's a point that needs litigating, we'll be in no condition to worry about it.

Pecksniff
I'll invest everything in this. I want a good slice of the pie.

Jonas
How much is everything?

Pecksniff
About a half million pounds.

Jonas
Sorry, not enough.

Montague
But, Jonas.

Jonas
No. No I say. It's too small. Why should we let him in for that amount?

Montague
Have you lost your mind? (Whispering.)

Jonas
No. Can't do it, Pecksniff, unless you cough up more.

Pecksniff
But I haven't any more.

Jonas
Can't be helped. Borrow it.

Pecksniff
How much?

Jonas
Oh, say another million.

Pecksniff
But where can I get that? Who would lend?

Jonas
Why, you're Old Martin's secretary, ain't you? Borrow some of his. In fact, all of his.

Montague
Jonas, you're a genius.

Pecksniff
But that would be dishonest.

Jonas
If you want to preach, all right. I thought you were a businessman.

Pecksniff
You're sure it's a sound investment?

Jonas
Of course.

Pecksniff
Then I'll do it. But what if—?

Jonas
Look, you buy the stock with his money and your own, of course. If you're short, simply pledge the stock to us, and we'll give you enough to cover it. It's a sure thing. In six months you'll be richer than Old Martin and he'll be no poorer.

Montague
Well, have you considered?

Pecksniff
Count me in. A penny saved is a penny earned.

Jobling
I propose a toast to our new partner?

All
Hear! Hear!

Jonas
Oh, by the way, Montague, it occurs to me we could use one more partner.

Montague
Who?

Jonas
A chap I know who lives in the country. In a couple of weeks we

must go to see him. Fabulously rich.

Montague
We can make a killing?

Jonas
Yes, if you're there, we can make a killing! But I can't do it without you.

Montague
Ah, but perhaps we've had enough.

Jonas
This fish is too big to let go I tell you. Millions, millions!

Montague
Ah, but I don't like traveling alone.

Jonas
Yes, but I'll be there.

Pecksniff
Yes, do it, Mr. Montague.

Montague
Very well, I will.

Jobling
To another killing.

All
Hurray.

Jobling
Cigar, Pecksniff—? No—injudicious.

BLACKOUT/CURTAIN

ACT II
SCENE 6

Mercy's Rooms.

Mercy
Is he better?

Prig
He ain't no worse. It's about the tenth time you've asked this hour.

Mercy
Oh, Mrs. Prig, if he regains consciousness you must come to me at once. You see, Mrs. Prig, I—this gentleman is my fiancé. Mr. Nadgett found him about ten miles from town in a swamp. He was left for dead. Nadgett is this gentleman's— confidential clerk. I'm sure there must have been foul play.

Prig
I'll tell you sure enough. But—

Mercy (eagerly)
Yes?

Prig
Where's my relief? (Sullen.)

Mercy

I think I hear her now? (Returns with Mrs. Gamp.) This is Mrs. Gamp. Mrs. Gamp—Mrs. Prig.

Gamp

The night nurse is well beknown to Mrs. Prig the day nurse, and the best of creatures. How is the poor dear gentleman tonight? If he ain't no better, what is expected must be prepared for. It ain't the first time by many a score that Mrs. Prig and me has nussed together. We knows each other's ways. Our charges is but low, ma'am, considerin' the nature of our painful dooties. If they was made accordin to our wishes, they would be easy paid.

Mercy

I'll leave you to your work. But Mrs. Gamp, you must not tell Mr. Jonas you are nursing a man.

Gamp

Never fear. Just a lying in.

(Mercy goes.)

Prig

I began to think you warn't coming.

Gamp

If perverse people go off dead when they is least expected, it ain't no fault of mine. How is the patient?

Prig

It ain't no matter what you say. His wits is gone.

Gamp

I hope the doctor left some instructions.

Prig

Oh, you're for a talking about it, are you! Well, I hope you get over it for I ain't interested in it myself.

Gamp

That was my way of askin' for anything you want to tell me.

Prig

The pickled salmon is quite delicious. I can particular recommend it. Meats taste of the stable, but the drinks is all good.

Gamp

Cowcumbers?

Prig

Ain't none.

Gamp

I knowed she wouldn't have a cowcumber. (Sniffs at some of the bowls.)

Prig

And don't go a dropping none of your snuff in it. In grue, barley water—apple tea—mutton broth and that, it don't signify. It stimulates the patient but I don't relish it myself.

Gamp

How can you talk so?

Prig

What, ain't your patients, wotever their disease is, always a sneezin' their heads off, along of your snuff.

Gamp

And wot if they are?

Prig
Nothing if they are, but don't deny it, Sairah.

Gamp
Who denies it? Who denies of it? (Darkly) Who denies of it, Betsey?

Prig
Nobody, if you don't, Sarah!

Gamp (Mollified.)
Betsey. I will now propoge a toast. (She pours tea.) My frequent partner, Betsey Prig.

Prig
Which altering the name to Sairah Gamp, I drink.

Gamp (Holding her hand up.)
No, Betsey. Drink fair wotever you do. Mrs. Harris was wont to say—

Prig
I'm glad of that.

Gamp
Why should you be glad of that, Betsey. She is unbeknown to you except by hearsay. If you have any think to say contrary to the character of Mrs. Harris, which well I knows is not to be impeaged behind her back or afore her face. Out with it, Betsey.

Prig
Bother, Mrs. Harris. I don't believe there no sich person!

Gamp
What! Have I knowed Mrs. Harris five and thirty year to be

told at last there ain't no sech person livin. But well mayn't you believe there's such a person, for she wouldn't demean herself to look at you, an often she has said when I have made mention of your name. Which to my sinful sorrow I have done, what, Sairey Gamp! Debarge yourself to her! Go along with you!

Prig
I'm a-goin', ma'am, ain't I? (She stops.)

Gamp
You had better, ma'am.

Prig
Do you know who you're talking to, ma'am?

Gamp
Apparently to Betsey Prig. Aperently so. I know her. No one better. Go along with you, do.

Prig
I blush for you.

Gamp
You had better blush a little for yourself.

Prig
We shall see how you get on without me. As for the physic, it's on the mantle shelf.

Gamp
I don't need you to tell me. I don't use it anyway.

Prig
And the armchair ain't comfortable. You'll want his piller. (Exit Betsey Prig)

Gamp

Deuce take your imperence. She has abuged me bein' in liquor, which I thought I smelt her even come. But not bein' used to it myself, I didn't believe it. But I could have bore it with a thankful hart. But the words she spoke of Mrs. Harris, lamb could not forgive. No Betsey. Nor worms forget. That perfeegus wretch. That I should hear from that same woman's lips what I have heard her speak of Mrs. Harris.

(Mercy enters.)

Mercy

Is anything wrong, Mrs. Gamp?

Gamp

I have had a happy deliverance from that woman Betsey Prig.

Mercy

Why?

Gamp

The torters she inflicts on her patients is frightful.

Mercy

You should have told me.

Gamp

Oh, Betsey Prig, wot wickedness you've shamed this night, but never shall you darken Sairey's doors again, you twening serpiant.

Mercy

But you were her friend.

Gamp

That's what I thought. That's the cutteny part. The things she said of Mrs. Harris. That there ain't no sich a woman. And ain't she waiting for me this minute.

Mercy
Oh this is all too complicated for me. Have a little tea.

Gamp
It ain't tea.

Mercy
Physic of some sort, I suppose. Have a little.

Gamp
On condition Betsey Prig never does another turn with me.

Mercy
Very well. Good night. Wake me if anything develops.

(Mercy goes looking tenderly at Montague.)

Gamp
I wonder if she forgot her bottle. (She settles down. Is uncomfortable. She gets up and takes Montague's pillow unceremoniously.) A little dull but not as bad ad might be. (She looks at Montague.) Ah, he'd make a lovely corpse. I'd so enjoy washing him down. Yet if he was to recover, why some men reward their nurses (with a wink) royally. (She sets tea for herself. Calls the chambermaid.) (Enter chambermaid.) Miss. I think, young woman, that I could pick a little bit of pickled salmon. I takes new bread, my dear, with just a little pat of fresh butter and a morsel of cheese. In case there should be such a thing as a cowcumber in the house would you be so kind as to bring it. They does a world of good in a sick room. And some ale. It bein considered wakeful by the doctors. That is my allowance and I never takes a drop beyond. Look sharp. Now. (Maid goes.) Ah what a blessed thing it is to

be contented to make the sick happy. Never mind oneself as long as one can do a service. (Enter maid.) I don't believe a finer cowcumber ever growed. I'm sure I never see one.

Montague
Ahhh.

Gamp
Ech. I thought he was a sleepen too pleasant to last. Don't make none oh that noise here. (To the maid.) You're desterbin' the patient.

(Maid goes.)

Montague
No. No—Don't—

Gamp
Oh, this is going to go on all night. Well I won't put up with it; I won't.

Montague
No. (In terror.)

Gamp
We looks charming. (Examining him) A deal charminger than we are. We needs a bath. Well, if I can't sleep I might as well give him a bath.

Montague (Screaming)
Don't do it.

Gamp (Takes the bowl and a sponge)
He wouldn't be washed if he had his own way. What a man. (Starts washing him.)

Montague (Momentarily lucid)
Don't put soap in my mouth.

Gamp
Couldn't you keep it shut then? If you wants to be tittivated, you must pay accordin'.

Montague
Leave me alone. (Wildly)

Gamp
What a way to conduct yourself. Instead of being grateful for all our little ways. For shame. (She uncovers him and washes his chest and the parts that there adjacent lie.) Take the man. Mrs. Prig's bottle. I thought he had her bottle there. My, what a man.

(Montague groans.)

Gamp
You don't like that. You just ain't hoomin. Well, I'll brush your hair. (She grabs him by the chin and rasps his hair with a hair brush.) I suppose you don't like that neither?

(Montague groans.)

Gamp (Triumphantly.)
Ah, I knowed you wouldn't.

(Enter Mercy.)

Mercy
Oh, Mrs. Gamp, is he awake?

Gamp
He's awake, but he ain't right in his head. He hates his nurses to

this hour. If you could have heard the poor, dear soul a findin fault with me you would have wondered how I stand it.

Mercy
Oh Montague, Montague speak to me. It is I, Mercy.

Montague
Who—how says the one.

Mercy
Oh this is horrible.

Montague
Don't do it—Jonas.

Mercy
Oh, Montague.

Montague
The Montagues and the Capulets are mortal enemies. I am a Montague.

Mercy
Montague, you must recognize me.

Montague
Mercy.

Mercy
At last.

Montague
Mercy, where are you?

Mercy
Right here.

Montague

Go way. You're not Mercy. You're my nurse. You can't fool me. I can tell you apart anywhere. Mercy. Mercy is big and stout and has a beard. You're not Mercy. Mercy was here a minute ago. She gave me a hand *bath*.

Mercy

He's confused us completely.

Montague

Merry. Merry. MERRY. Ah. (He wakes up.) Oh Merry. I just had the most horrible nightmare. (He sees Sairey Gamp.) No. No it wasn't—it can't be. Help!

Mercy

Everything's all right, darling. Darling, what happened?

Montague

Nothing much. Jonas tried to kill me, that's all. He told me we we're going to see a rich eccentric who lived in the country. Like a fool I went. He bungled the job.

Mercy

What are we going to do?

Montague

I'll fix him. You are allowed but one shot at murder. Get Nadgett.

Mercy

Mrs. Gamp, call Mr. Nadgett.

Montague

What's he doing here? How did I get here? Above all how did she get here?

Mercy
Nadgett found you. He followed you and then brought you here to avoid notice. Mrs. Gamp is your nurse.

Montague
How long have I been here?

Mercy
A week.

Montague
Good heavens. We've got to work fast.

(Enter Nadgett.)

Montague
Nadgett, you are my good angel. Drop explanations. Go round up Pecksniff, Jonas and Old Martin and Charity. Bring them here. Use any pretext. But don't explain why. Unless you have something further to add; go.

(Nadgett registers approval and leaves hurriedly.)

Montague
That man is invaluable.

Mercy
Err, Montague I have a confession to make.

Montague
Yes.

Mercy
I don't think Nadgett will have to bring Old Martin around. He's coming here anyway. I, *uh*, invited him.

Montague
You mean you gave him an assignation?

Mercy
Yes. (Eagerly.) But this is the very first one. I couldn't hold out any longer, you see. I did it for your sake.

Montague
Oh, of course.

Mercy
I did, I really did. (Injured.)

Montague
Well, you wouldn't care too much if he got lost now would you?

Mercy
Of course not. (Slightly reluctant.)

Montague
Then call Mrs. Gamp.

(Mercy goes to the door and calls. Enter Mrs. Gamp.)

Montague
Mrs. Gamp how long has it been since—since you were last—err, in love?

Gamp
Why as I was saying to Mrs. Harris the other day, which I am always saying—it's been a long time.

Montague
Well would you care to meet a very eligible bachelor under propitious circumstances?

Gamp
Why, sir—you don't mean. You're a *royal* gentleman.

Montague (Understanding her suddenly. Aghast.)
No. Not what you think. Someone else.

Gamp
I thought he was a royal gentelman. Well I'm not as eager but I ain't unwillin.

Montague
Wonderful. Would you consent to receive him in the dark?

Gamp
In the dark?

Montague
Here—with no lights. In the bedroom.

Gamp
Why, sir?

Montague
Of course, I'll be here, to protect you.

Gamp
Oh but you don't need to do that. I ain't afraid of the dark.

Montague
No. no I dare say you're not.

Mercy
I think that must be him.

Montague
I'll run and hide. Ahh. I can't move. No good, I'll have to stay,

Mercy
Shall I let him in?

Montague
Yes. Now, Mrs. Gamp, you must pretend to be Mercy. He thinks she has given him an assignation. In the dark. You understand?

(Lights are dimmed.)

Gamp
I do. If only Mrs. Harris was here to see this.

Voice Off Stage
Here I am, Mercy.

Mercy
Well, so you are, old fright.

Old Martin
Not such a fright tonight, Mercy. Tonight I'm going to be jolly.

Mercy
Now first, take your clothes off. That's it, your pants, too. Now close your eyes. Spin around three times. Now you must find me. (She doses the lights)

Old Martin
Hey, what happened to the lights? I can't see a thing.

Mercy
That's part of the game. Here I am.

Old Martin
Jolly. (Enter Old Martin in waistcoat but with no pants.) Where are you, little bird?

(Gamp rustles her skirts.)

Old Martin
Tweet, tweet. I hear you flutter. (He walks about bumping into things, hands stretched before him. Finally he touches Sarah.) Hey, that felt like bristles; I must be in the wrong room. Jolly, pardon me, sir.

Sarah
Come here, old fright. (Imitating Mercy not too effectively.)

Old Martin
Oh, it is you. Well what did I just touch? You are at your old games. You make your voice sound like a man's. I know your tricks. Jolly. (He putters about. He finally is embraced by Gamp, back to audience.)

Old Martin
Help. Let me go. Do you want to pull it off.

Gamp
Shh, darling; the bed's over here.

Old Martin
Bed. You won't catch me in bed with your old sodmite legs.

Gamp
Hush.

Old Martin
It must be a witch. Help. Help a witch.

Gamp
Well, if you're going to take on like that there's no help for it. I must save my honor. Rape, rape.

(Enter Pecksniff, cautiously.)

Pecksniff
Did someone call for help? (He opens the door but very little light is let in.)

Gamp
Rape!

Pecksniff
Let it never be said that I refused to defend one of the fairer sex. (He struggles with both of them.) If there was only some light. I can't tell which is which. Ah, soft skin here. Bristles there. Bristles avaunt. (He wallops Mrs. Gamp.)

Gamp
What are you doin? (She wallops Pecksniff.)

Pecksniff
Rapist. (He punches her.)

(Gamp falls on Pecksniff and flattens him. Meanwhile, Old Martin has got loose and dodges about. Mercy enters with a lamp. Pecksniff is on the floor. Old Martin is disheveled near the bed.)

Mercy
What is going on here?

Gamp
Oh, Miss Mercy, there are two villains whats as has tried to rape me.

Pecksniff
No, no, I came to help you. Excuse me, please, I thought you were a witch.

Old Martin
Pecksniff, I'm sure you can explain this.

Mercy
Perhaps you'd better explain where you left your pants, Mr. Chuzzlewit.

Old Martin
What. Jolly! But you know very well where I left them.

Mercy
I. I know anything about it. Are you serious?

Old Martin
Oh ho. Jolly, I see how the land lies.

Pecksniff
Oh, Martin, Martin, this does not look well.

Old Martin (Jumps into bed and then jumps out aghast.)
There's a body in that bed.

Pecksniff
A body? Why, it's Mr. Montague.

Gamp
He was alive afore you murderers came here.

Old Martin
Looks dead to me. And his name is Tigg.

Pecksniff
No, no. He's the head of the Anglo American Loan Co. How did he come here?

Old Martin
How did you come here?

Pecksniff
Why, to see my daughter.

Old Martin
That's a pretty lame excuse.

Pecksniff
And what are you doing here?

Old Martin
I came to see Miss Pecksniff.

Pecksniff
You came to see my daughter, like that? Come now. It won't do.

Old Martin
I came by invitation.

Mercy
What *are* you talking about?

Pecksniff
You see: whereas I did? Nothing suspicious about visiting my daughter.

Mercy
But I didn't ask you to come, Papa.

Pecksniff
But, darling, you're not angry with me? You will have your fun. Such a playful child. Just because I pretend to throw her out. You don't bear a grudge about that, do you?

Mercy
Why, of course not, Papa. But truth is the truth.

Old Martin
Well, Pecksniff, this is jolly.

Pecksniff
But why should I want to harm Mr. Montague? I'm a shareholder in his concern.

Old Martin
Precisely why you should want to kill Mr. Tigg. Because it's a swindle, that's why. You've lost everything you put in.

Pecksniff
But that's impossible: it was a sure thing.

Old Martin
Look here, I know this man's name is Tigg. Montague's his first name but for business purposes—to wit: swindle—he changed it around.

Pecksniff
You mean I've been had?

Old Martin
Precisely. I set him up to swindle you all.

Pecksniff
Jolly. Ha ha ha.

Old Martin
You think it funny?

Pecksniff
Yes, because, you see, he persuaded me to steal all your invest-

ments and put them into the capital stock. And, of course, I did because I thought it a sound business venture.

Old Martin
You blithering idiot.

Pecksniff
Now it seems you have a motive, too. There are liabilities, you know. You can't get your money back. You're as poor as a church mouse cousin.

Old Martin
Why you, you.

Pecksniff
Temper, temper.

Old Martin
But, wait a minute. What is he doing here at Mercy's lodgings?

Montague
Why, gentlemen, that's easily explained.

(General consternation from Old Martin and Pecksniff.)

Montague
I was brought here by Nadgett who found me where Cousin Jonas had left me for dead.

Pecksniff
Well that clears me. And, you, too, damn it.

Montague
Why, Pecksniff, have you given up the idea of inheriting Old Martin's Fortune?

Old Martin
Yes, Pecksniff.

Montague
And, Mr. Chuzzlewit, haven't you abandoned the idea of defrauding your relatives?

Pecksniff
Two can play at that.

Old Martin
Why should I worry? You'll have to give it back to me, Tigg.

Montague
Have to, Martin?

Old Martin
Of course.

Pecksniff
And mine, too?

Montague
Why, of course?

Old Martin
Because if you don't, I'll call the police.

Pecksniff
Precisely. If you don't, we call the police.

Montague
Police? I shouldn't think you'd want to deal with them. Would you think so, Mrs. Gamp?

Gamp
No.

Montague
Or you, Mercy?

Mercy
Hardly.

Old Martin
What is this?

Pecksniff
Yes. Is this some kind of double cross?

Montague
I believe it is given that name in the vernacular.

Old Martin
You can't get away with this. I have too much money to be suspected.

Pecksniff
And I, as a man of the cloth, have too much prestige.

Old Martin
You are nothing, Tigg. I'll put you back in the gutter where I found you.

Pecksniff
It won't do.

Montague
May I point out to you, Martin, that thanks to Pecksniff here you have no money worth speaking of. And you, Pecksniff, as well as you, Martin, won't have too much prestige left

after you are arrested for rape. A hanging offense in these parts.

(Pecksniff and Martin look at each other aghast, and then at Gamp and Mercy. Gamp and Mercy nod smiling.)

Pecksniff
But, I'm your father.

Mercy
And I'm going to act like *your* daughter. (She smiles.) I must defend truth. Even if it sends poor Pa to the gallows.

Old Martin
But you ain't mad at me, are you? I'm jolly.

Mercy
Angry. Of course, not. I'm sure you're a sweet old thing and just came here without your pants as a joke. I hope the jury will think so.

Montague
You see, the game is up. You look bilious, my dear Martin,—if so, water as the doctor would say. Yes, I can see you feel the halter tighten. Very well then. I keep the money and you keep quiet.

Old Martin
But, it's not fair.

Montague
Would you prefer justice? (Makes a hanging motion.)

Old Martin
Just gives us some, a little bit.

Montague
Well, now to show I'm not a complete spoil sport, I will provide for you.

Pecksniff
That's handsome.

Old Martin
Jolly.

Montague
Mercy and I plan to be married. Now, first I must settle accounts with Jonas. Martin, will you go put your pants on, please. He should be here presently.

(Old Martin goes out and returns presently with trousers. Puts them on as Tigg speaks.)

Montague
You like to play the moral misanthrope, Martin. I'm going to pretend to be dead. When Jonas gets here you must accuse him of my murder. Make him squirm.

Old Martin
I know my part.

Jonas (Outside.)
Look here, Nadgett. I don't half like this.

Nadgett
You'll be interested in the result. Just be patient.

Jonas
I shouldn't be out here but for you. What are we stopping for now?

Nadgett
Here we are.

Jonas
Hallo. There are enough of you here. (Nadgett closes the door and braces himself against it.) What is *all* this?

(Old Martin motions towards the body.)

Jonas
What's the matter? Is anybody hurt? Don't seem so. Cuts and bruises, we've all got them.

Old Martin
He's dead. If you attempt to leave, we'll fling up the window and call for help.

Jonas
What is all this? So, he's dead. I never heard you were his father or had any particular reason to care much about him.

Nadgett
You murdered him.

Jonas
I? Have you any proof?

Nadgett
I followed you. Though I didn't actually see you.

Jonas
You. Who will take your word?

Nadgett
And a further witness that you killed your father.

Jonas
Who?

Nadgett
Mr. Chuffy.

Jonas
But he's an idiot.

Chuffy (Enters.)
Who lies dead upstairs? (Vacantly.)

Jonas
No one will believe him.

Pecksniff
Are you so sure?

Old Martin
Did Jonas poison his father, Mr. Chuffy?

Chuffy
He bought poison. I saw him put it in the draw. Then I took it out. He thought he poisoned him. Your own son, Mr. Chuzzlewit.

Jonas
Well. Are you satisfied?

Montague
Not quite. (He rises to a sitting posture.)

Jonas
No. You're dead, I killed you.

Montague
Not quite. Jonas, did it ever occur to you that you have no talent? That you're a buffoon, pure and simple. Well, let me be the first to inform you. You can't even commit murder without a mishap. You not only don't escape, you don't even do the deed properly.

Jonas
But, it looks as though I do escape. You daren't testify against me. And Chuffy's testimony clears me of killing the old ghost. God it feels good to call him that again. I didn't when I thought I'd killed him.

Montague
But who will believe Mr. Chuffy?

Jonas
What?

Montague
He's an imbecile. And we've traced the apothecary, haven't we, Nadgett.

Nadgett
That's right. There's enough circumstantial evidence to hang you.

Jonas
What must I do?

Montague
I mean to be revenged, Jonas.

Jonas
What are you going to do?

Montague
Nadgett.

(Nadgett opens the door and in comes Charity. She confers in whispers with Montague.)

Mercy
Why, hello Charity.

Charity
And how are you, Mercy?

Mercy
Fine.

Charity
Jonas, sweet child, bring me a chair.

(Jonas stands stupefied for a moment.)

Jonas
Can't you get it yourself?

Montague
Bring the lady a chair, Jonas. It won't be the last you'll ever bring her.

Charity
I believe you have met my fiancé before?

Jonas
But I'm not your—her fiancé.

Montague
Jonas, you are her fiancé. Soon you will be her husband. Don't contradict her. It's very impolite. I have just confided your

secret to her.

Jonas
This ain't handsome, Montague. This ain't handsome.

Charity
I am sure that I ought to be very grateful for the blessings I enjoy, and those that are yet in store for me. When I contrast Jonas' devotion with what other women have for husbands and when I think that in the dispensations of this world—oh, I have much to be thankful for—and much to make me humble and contented. Of course, I don't want any *more* revenge. Why, Jonas, what is the cause of your appearance of depression? Are you of a melancholy? It must be because I refused you so many times. No, don't speak. You won't be able to before other company. I *was cruel*. He has never recovered from that cruelty. What right had I to refuse him three times? I was wrong. Merry, if you ever feel toward a person the way I really feel towards him, at that feeling find expressing.

(They all stare at her. Montague with satisfaction.)

Old Martin
Jolly.

Charity
Jonas! My fan.

(Jonas brings the fan. His look is a desperate one.)

Pecksniff (Piously)
I could wish you and Merry were better friends.

Charity
Every relation of life is now bound up and cemented in Jonas. So

long as he is my own, I cannot want a friend. I bear no malice at any time toward anyone, much less toward my sister.

(Meanwhile, Jonas goes to Montague.)

Jonas
You're sure you wouldn't prefer to prosecute. I haven't got the guts myself, but if you were to prosecute I—I shouldn't complain. I'd endeavor to hang like a man.

Montague
Sorry, Jonas. I want my revenge. I say, look out there. I wonder that in these crowded streets the foot passengers aren't oftener run over.

Jonas (Bitterly.)
The drivers won't do it.

Montague
Do you mean—?

Jonas
There are some men (lugubriously) who can't get run over. They lead a charmed life. Coal wagons recoil from them and even cabs refuse to run them down. Aye, there are such men. One of them is a friend of mine.

Charity
Come, Jonas, child. You may escort me home.

(Jonas looks to Montague beseechingly. But he goes.)

Montague
I almost pity him.

Pecksniff
Now that he's gone what about us?

Old Martin
Yes, us?

Montague
I have the very thing for you Martin. Mrs. Gamp.

Old Martin
What does this mean?

Montague
This means you must have a cup of tea with Mrs. Gamp.

Old Martin
I won't do it.

Montague
But Mrs. Gamp is going to receive a pension from me for her part in this affair. Roughly a million dollars.

Old Martin
I'll do it.

Pecksniff
And me, Montague?

Mercy
Why, Daddy, I think I know the very thing.

Pecksniff
Really, what?

Mercy
Old Martin is not quite enough for a woman as youthful as Mrs.

Gamp.

Pecksniff
Why, gad, that's true. And besides, I can preach a sermon afterwards that will make your hair stand on end. Egad, hers does anyway.

Gamp
I says to Mrs. Harris the other day—there's some happy creaturs that time runs backward with—you are one.

(Montague and Mercy hugging each other as Gamp embraces her harem.)

Jolly!

CURTAIN

ABOUT THE AUTHOR

Frank J. Morlock has written and translated many plays since retiring from the legal profession in 1992. His translations have also appeared on Project Gutenberg, the Alexandre Dumas Père web page, Literature in the Age of Napoléon, Infinite Artistries.com, and Munsey's (formerly Blackmask). In 2006 he received an award from the North American Jules Verne Society for his translations of Verne's plays. He lives and works in México.

www.ingramcontent.com/pod-product-compliance
Lightning Source LLC
LaVergne TN
LVHW041622070426
835507LV00008B/407